COOKING WITH
Bon Appétit

COOKING WITH
Bon Appétit

Appetizers

THE KNAPP PRESS
Publishers
Los Angeles

Copyright © 1982 by Knapp Communications Corporation

Published by The Knapp Press
5900 Wilshire Boulevard, Los Angeles, California 90036

Library of Congress Cataloging in Publication Data
Main entry under title:
Cooking with Bon appétit.

    Includes index.
    1. Cookery (Appetizers) I. Bon appétit.
II. Title: Appetizers.
TX740.C657   1982   641.8'12   82-13083
ISBN 0-89535-105-6

On the cover: *(clockwise from top left)* Quick Piroshki, Smoked Salmon Rolls, *Herring-Stuffed Beets, Pickled Mushrooms*

Printed and bound in the United States of America

10 9 8

🍒 Contents

Foreword . . . . *vii*

1 Dips, Mousses and Pâtés 1
  Dips and Spreads 2
  Vegetable Pâtés, Terrines and Mousses 9
  Seafood Pâtés, Terrines and Mousses 16
  Poultry and Meat Pâtés and Terrines 21

2 Salads and Cold Platters 27
  Vegetables and Fruits 28
  Seafood 35
  Poultry 39
  Meats 42
  Grains 46

3 Cold Hors d'Oeuvres 47
  Stuffed Vegetables 48
  Marinated and Pickled Vegetables 52
  Eggs and Cheese 54
  Seafood 56
  Meats 57
  Nuts 57

4 Pastries, Canapés and Breads . . . 59
  Pastries   60
  Canapés, Croustades and Sandwiches   68
  Breads, Crackers and Chips   73

5 Hot Appetizers 81
  Vegetables and Cheese   82
  Seafood   89
  Poultry   93
  Meats   96

6 Drinks 109

  Index 115

🍃 Foreword

No course of a meal offers more exciting variety than appetizers. They range from smoothly pureed spreads and mousses to hearty pâtés and cold cuts, dainty stuffed eggs and vegetables to crisp tartlets and fritters, spicy kebabs of seafood or poultry to meatballs in a tangy sauce. Almost every kind of ingredient, every cooking method, can be used to make dishes whose sole aim is to delight the appetite and whet it for the meal to follow.

More than 200 such delightful first-course recipes have been gathered here from the pages of *Bon Appétit*. For your convenience in planning a meal, they have been organized into five chapters: spreadable appetizers, salads, cold hors d'oeuvres or "finger foods," appetizers based on pastries and breads, and hot dishes. A sixth chapter offers a selection of the cocktails and punches that sometimes precede or accompany appetizers.

In addition, each chapter of the book includes features on specific aspects of cooking and serving appetizers. In the first chapter, for example, you will find instructions for preparing, storing and serving pâtés (pages 14–15). The chapter on pastries and breads includes guidelines for handling tissue-thin Greek phyllo dough (pages 65 and 67) and making canapés (page 69). And the drinks chapter offers hints on selecting a first-course wine (page 110) and preparing a party punch bowl (page 112).

When you select an appetizer, it always helps to bear in mind the rest of the menu. The first course should complement or pleasingly contrast with the courses that follow and should not repeat any of the dominant ingredients or flavors. The occasion, the season and—above all—your imagination will help you in your choice. One very successful form of entertaining, however, does not even require that you choose a single first course. A buffet of hot and cold appetizers is a perfect way to serve large gatherings with a minimum of fuss—particularly because many appetizers can be made in advance.

And it can be fun to plan your appetizer buffet around an international theme. Virtually every one of the world's major cuisines has some kind of appetizer buffet—Russian *zakuski*, French *hors d'oeuvres variés*, Italian *antipasti*, Greek *mezes*, Spanish *tapas*, Swedish *smörgåsbord*—and you will find many examples of each of these specialties throughout the book. Served with the native drink, be it wine, beer, vodka, ouzo or aquavit, your appetizer buffet will be as successful as it is easy to prepare.

1 ❦ Dips, Mousses and Pâtés

Spreadable appetizers are a marvelous asset for the busy host or hostess. They are incomparably easy to make and, in most cases, they can be whipped up and stored days in advance of a party. Served with an assortment of breads, crackers, chips or vegetables, they have great visual appeal. And there is something wonderfully satisfying about spreading and eating bite after bite of a smooth dip, mousse or pâté.

You can combine virtually any ingredients to make a good dip, but these simplest of spreadable appetizers usually feature light main ingredients—vegetables, cheeses and seafood—combined with lively seasonings and a creamy base such as mayonnaise, cream, sour cream or yogurt. Usually they are served thoroughly chilled, but a notable exception is Chile con Queso (page 2), a Mexican dip of molten cheese vibrantly flavored with onion, garlic, chili powder, tomatoes and jalapeño peppers.

"Mousse" means "froth" in French: many of these spreadables are bound with whipped cream which, when the mousse is molded and chilled, sets it firmly to make an especially attractive presentation. Even when whipped cream is not included, a mousse will be made with an abundance of some thick, smooth ingredient such as sour cream or mayonnaise, along with gelatin to help the mixture set. Seafood is best suited to this superbly light variety of appetizer, and often several kinds are combined to make an elaborate molded mousse such as the one on page 17.

Pâtés of meat or poultry have been around for centuries, making a slow transition from the French farmhouse kitchen to the elegant tables of *haute cuisine* restaurants. In their most traditional form, they are encased in a pastry crust before cooking (the word "pâté," in fact, refers to the pastry). But most of what we call pâtés today are actually terrines, pureed and chopped meat mixtures baked in an earthenware dish (*terrine* in French) or other heatproof container. For all the rich and complex flavor of a classic Country Pâté (page 22), these hearty spreadables are still quite easy to prepare (see box, pages 14–15). And the new wave that has swept the kitchens of France has left its mark on these dishes too: on pages 9–21 you will find a wide array of pâtés and terrines made exclusively with vegetables and seafood—appetizers at once light and yet substantial enough to stand on their own as a luncheon or picnic main course.

 Dips and Spreads

Herb Dip

Makes about 2 cups

1 cup cottage cheese
½ cup mayonnaise
¼ cup sour cream
1 garlic clove, minced
1 tablespoon minced onion
2 teaspoons chopped fresh parsley

1 teaspoon Worcestershire sauce
1 teaspoon chopped chives
½ teaspoon salt
Dash of hot pepper sauce
Assorted crudités

Combine all ingredients except crudités in medium bowl and mix well. Cover and refrigerate overnight. Serve with assorted crudités.

Chile con Queso

Serve from a chafing dish as a dip for taco chips.

Makes about 4 cups

1 tablespoon vegetable oil
1 large onion, chopped
1 garlic clove, minced
1 tablespoon all purpose flour
1 tablespoon chili powder or to taste
1 10-ounce can tomatoes and green chilies or 1 16-ounce can whole tomatoes mixed with ¼ cup diced green chilies

1 pound processed American cheese, cut into 1-inch cubes
2 jalapeño peppers (or to taste), seeded and chopped
Homemade Taco Chips (see recipe, page 80)

Heat oil in 3-quart saucepan over medium heat. Add onion and garlic and sauté until onion is translucent, about 5 minutes. Stir in flour and chili powder and cook, stirring constantly, 1 minute. Add tomatoes and chilies and continue cooking until thickened, about 5 to 6 minutes. Reduce heat to low and gradually add cheese, stirring constantly until cheese is completely melted. Stir in peppers. Taste and adjust seasoning. Serve hot with Homemade Taco Chips.

Avocado-Yogurt Dip

4 to 6 servings

1 cup plain yogurt
1 large ripe avocado, peeled, seeded and coarsely chopped
2 shallots, chopped
1 green onion, chopped

½ teaspoon dried tarragon or 1½ teaspoons minced fresh tarragon
Pinch of oregano
Lemon juice
Salt and freshly ground pepper

Combine all ingredients in processor or blender and mix until smooth.
Dip can be prepared 1 day ahead.

Crudités with Peruvian Peanut Dipping Sauce

Makes 3 cups

1 tablespoon butter
1 large onion, sliced
3 garlic cloves, sliced
1¾ to 2 cups chicken consommé
¾ cup peanut butter
1 tablespoon whipping cream
1 tablespoon fresh lime juice
1 small green chili, finely chopped
   or 1 tablespoon *each* minced
   green bell pepper and chili
   powder

Cherry tomatoes
Thinly sliced jícama
Trimmed and blanched asparagus

Melt butter in large skillet over medium-high heat. Add onion and garlic and sauté until browned, about 10 to 15 minutes. Reduce heat and stir in 1¾ cups consommé with peanut butter, whipping cream, lime juice and chili. Simmer about 10 minutes. Transfer to processor or blender and puree until smooth, adding remaining consommé if mixture seems too thick. Transfer to serving bowl, cover and chill.

To serve, arrange dipping sauce in center of large platter and surround with tomatoes, jícama and asparagus.

Snow Peas with Lemon-Anchovy Dipping Sauce

Can be prepared several days ahead. Make sure all sauce ingredients are at room temperature before combining them.

Makes about 1¼ cups

Dipping Sauce
2 egg yolks
3 to 4 tablespoons Dijon mustard
1 2-ounce can anchovies, undrained
   Juice of 1 lemon or to taste
1 shallot, chopped
1 cup vegetable oil
¼ cup sour cream (optional)
   Salt and freshly ground pepper

1 tablespoon capers, rinsed and
   drained
   Additional capers (optional
   garnish)

1¼ pounds fresh snow peas or 2
   pounds small, young sugar snap
   peas

Combine egg yolks, mustard, anchovies, lemon juice and shallot in processor and mix until foamy and pale. With machine running, slowly drizzle in oil, stopping occasionally to make sure oil is being absorbed. If sauce is very stiff, mix in sour cream. Season with salt and pepper. Turn into storage container. Stir in capers. Cover and refrigerate until shortly before serving. Top with capers if desired.

String snow peas or sugar snaps and crisp in ice water. Drain well and arrange in sunburst pattern on flat basket. Place bowl of dipping sauce in center.

Variation: If fresh snow peas or sugar snap peas are not available, substitute carrot sticks and cauliflower florets. Garnish with green onion tops for color.

Any leftover peas can be added to salads or sautéed with chopped ham and green onion for an attractive side dish.

Remaining dipping sauce can be thinned with oil and vinegar and flavored with garlic for salad dressing.

Raw Radish Sauce

8 to 10 servings

1 cup finely chopped radishes
1 8-ounce package cream cheese, room temperature
1 garlic clove, minced
1 tablespoon fresh lemon juice
¾ teaspoon salt

½ teaspoon dried dillweed
Dash of freshly ground pepper
Parsley sprigs and radish slices (garnish)
Assorted crudités

Combine first 6 ingredients and mix well. Season with pepper. Turn into serving dish, cover and chill 4 hours. Garnish with parsley and radish slices and serve with assorted crudités.

Perfect Guacamole

There seem to be more versions of guacamole than there are avocados in this world. Our recipe follows traditional precepts—the mixture must be chunky (never a puree), have bite from fresh chilies and be perfumed with fresh coriander. The addition of garlic is optional, but lime juice is necessary. Vary this according to taste.

4 to 6 servings

2 tablespoons minced onion
1 to 2 serrano chilies,* seeded and coarsely chopped (begin with a little and add more to taste)
1 garlic clove, minced (optional)
2 teaspoons chopped fresh coriander (do not substitute ground coriander as it has a completely different flavor)

Juice of ½ lime
2 large ripe avocados, halved, seeded and peeled
1 large tomato, peeled, seeded and chopped
Salt
Lime juice
Homemade Taco Chips (see recipe, page 80)

Combine 1½ tablespoons onion with chilies, garlic, coriander and lime juice in processor and chop using on/off turns until semi-pureed. Turn into mixing bowl. Add avocado and mash with fork. Add tomato and remaining onion and toss to blend. Season to taste with salt and lime juice. Serve at room temperature with Homemade Taco Chips.

Can be prepared several hours ahead and refrigerated. Sprinkle guacamole with lime juice to prevent darkening.

*Serrano chilies are very hot. Be careful when handling as oils may burn skin; wash hands immediately after handling. If milder taste is preferred, substitute green chilies. If fresh chilies are unavailable, use canned chilies.

Taramosalata

Makes about 2½ cups

2 slices firm bread (1½ ounces total), crusts trimmed
½ cup cold water
1 large russet potato (10 ounces), cooked, cooled to room temperature, peeled and shredded

½ cup tarama* (Greek carp roe)
3 tablespoons fresh lemon juice
1 cup oil (preferably safflower)
Assorted crudités

Soak bread thoroughly in water; squeeze dry. Combine with potato, tarama and lemon juice in processor, or in batches in blender, and mix well. With machine running, drizzle in oil until mixture thickens. Check thickness after all oil is added; if necessary blend in ¼ cup water to thin to dipping consistency. Serve with assorted crudités.

*Tarama is available in Greek markets.

Crabmeat Dip

Makes about 2½ cups

¾ cup mayonnaise
1 6-ounce can crabmeat, rinsed, drained and refreshed with 1 teaspoon fresh lemon juice
⅓ cup finely chopped green pepper
⅓ cup seeded, chopped and drained tomato

1 teaspoon chopped green onion (white part only)
Freshly ground pepper or ground red pepper
Crackers

Combine all ingredients except crackers in medium bowl and mix well. Transfer to serving bowl. Cover and chill. Serve dip on platter surrounded with crackers.

Crabmeat Paste

6 servings

1 6-ounce can crabmeat
¼ cup chopped almonds
¼ cup olive oil
2 tablespoons minced fresh parsley

¼ teaspoon salt
2 tablespoons dry white wine
Toast rounds

Remove fiber and shell bits from crabmeat. Reserve a few larger pieces of crab to garnish the paste.

Sauté almonds in 2 tablespoons oil until light brown. Drain and let cool.

Mix crabmeat, almonds, parsley and salt in blender at low speed, slowly adding wine and remaining olive oil. Blend until smooth. Garnish with reserved crabmeat and chill.

Serve crabmeat paste on warm toast rounds.

Angel of Death Cheese

The Piedmontese are very fond of cheese. This recipe, with its head of garlic, is guaranteed to keep away the Angel of Death.

Makes about 1½ pints

1 large head of garlic, separated into cloves
8 ounces ricotta cheese, room temperature
4 ounces Gorgonzola cheese, crumbled, room temperature

1 cup whipping cream
¾ teaspoon salt
2 fresh sage leaves
⅓ cup walnuts, finely chopped
Assorted crackers

Add garlic to small saucepan of boiling water and cook until garlic is tender and easily pierced with knife, about 15 to 20 minutes. Drain well. Transfer to garlic press in batches and mince. Measure 2 tablespoons and set aside.

Beat ricotta in medium bowl until softened. Add Gorgonzola and continue mixing until smooth. Gradually beat in cream. Add salt and reserved garlic.

Dampen 12 × 18-inch piece of cheesecloth and wring dry. Arrange 2 sage leaves bottom side up in center. Spoon cheese mixture over leaves, forming loose ball. Tie ends of cloth together, pressing cheese mixture gently into shape. Transfer to cheesecloth-lined strainer and set strainer over bowl. Refrigerate 24 hours (or up to 4 days).

Unmold cheese onto platter. Press walnuts over entire surface. Refrigerate. Let stand at room temperature for 1 hour before serving. Accompany with an assortment of crackers.

Liptauer Cheese

Liptauer is almost as popular in Germany as it is in Austria and Hungary, where the tangy, fresh, sheep's milk cheese is sometimes substituted for cream cheese. Vary flavorings according to taste.

Mounded in a hollowed-out, rich brown pumpernickel loaf and surrounded by colorful garnishes, this rose-tinted, easy-to-do spread makes a spectacular presentation. Invite guests to spread the Liptauer on small squares of rye or black bread and then top with their choice of garnishes.

12 servings

1 pound 3 ounces cream cheese (preferably without preservatives), room temperature
6 ounces sharp cheddar cheese, room temperature
5 tablespoons unsalted butter, softened
1½ to 2 teaspoons Dijon mustard
2 tablespoons chopped onion
Sweet Hungarian paprika

1 round loaf pumpernickel bread about 14 to 16 inches in diameter*

Garnishes
2 cans anchovy fillets, rinsed and chopped
⅔ cup finely chopped green onion
⅔ cup finely chopped cucumber
⅔ cup diced radishes
½ cup drained capers
Small squares of pumpernickel, rye and black bread

Up to 4 days before serving (Liptauer must have time to mellow and should not be prepared less than 1 day ahead), combine cream cheese, cheddar, butter, mustard and onion in processor and blend until smooth. Add enough paprika to give a rosy color. (If using an electric mixer, chop cheddar into small dice and beat with other ingredients until smooth.) Cover and refrigerate.

To assemble, hollow out pumpernickel loaf by removing the top third (a round about 9 inches in diameter) and scooping out some of bread interior. (This bread can be reserved for crumbs.) Mound Liptauer in loaf, cover completely with plastic wrap and refrigerate. Place garnishes in small bowls or crocks, cover with plastic and refrigerate. Shortly before serving, place filled loaf on table, accompanied by one or two spreading knives, and surround with bowls or crocks and a basket of breads.

*May be ordered from bakery several days in advance.

Bleu Cheese Log

Makes about 2 cups

1 8-ounce package cream cheese, room temperature
1 4-ounce package bleu cheese (preferably Danish), room temperature
½ cup (1 stick) butter, room temperature

1 tablespoon brandy
½ cup minced fresh parsley
1 to 2 teaspoons poppy seed
Sliced black olives (garnish)
Fresh parsley sprigs (garnish)
Crackers

Combine first 4 ingredients in small bowl and mix until smooth, about 5 minutes. Shape into cylinder. Sprinkle large piece of foil or plastic wrap with ½ cup parsley and poppy seed. Place cylinder on top and roll to coat completely, using foil or plastic wrap as aid. Seal tightly. Chill at least 8 hours, preferably overnight. Arrange log on serving platter. Garnish with olives and parsley. Serve with crackers.

Baked Brie Spread

4 to 6 servings

1 8-ounce wheel Brie or
   Camembert
2 tablespoons (¼ stick) butter,
   room temperature

¼ cup sliced almonds
French bread, sliced apples or
pears

Preheat oven to 350°F. Set Brie in ovenproof serving dish. Spread butter over top. Arrange sliced almonds on butter. Bake until softened and heated through, about 12 to 15 minutes. Serve warm with bread, apples or pears.

Homemade Herb Cheese

This can be made ahead and chilled for up to three days.

Makes 2 cups

1 12-ounce package cream cheese,
   room temperature
½ cup (1 stick) butter, room
   temperature
3 large garlic cloves, minced
1 tablespoon minced chives
1½ teaspoons dried chervil, crumbled

1½ teaspoons dried tarragon,
   crumbled
1 teaspoon dried parsley, crumbled
½ teaspoon dried thyme, crumbled
¼ teaspoon freshly ground white
   pepper

Combine all ingredients in medium bowl and mix until smooth. Spoon into crock. Cover and chill. Bring to room temperature before serving.

Caponata (Italian Eggplant Appetizer)

6 to 8 servings

   Olive oil
1 medium eggplant, unpeeled and
   cut into 1-inch cubes

1 large onion, chopped
1 cup chopped fennel or celery
1 garlic clove, minced
   Handful of toasted pine nuts
¾ cup pitted green olives, coarsely
   chopped

⅓ cup drained chopped tomatoes or
   ¼ cup tomato sauce
3 tablespoons capers
2 tablespoons vinegar
   Pinch of sugar
   Salt and freshly ground pepper
   Lavash or Italian bread

Heat oil in large skillet over high heat. Add eggplant in batches and sauté until golden, adding oil as needed. Drain well on paper towels and set aside.
   Using same skillet, sauté onion, fennel, garlic and pine nuts, tossing lightly. Reduce heat to medium and add olives, tomatoes, capers, vinegar, sugar, salt and pepper; cook briefly over medium heat. Add eggplant and simmer until eggplant is tender, but fennel is still crunchy. Allow to cool slightly, then cover and chill well. Serve with lavash or Italian bread.

Eggplant Spread

Serve on cucumber rounds or whole wheat crackers.

8 to 12 servings

1 large eggplant
¼ cup minced green onion
2 teaspoons olive oil
2 teaspoons catsup

2 garlic cloves, mashed
1 teaspoon fresh lemon juice
1 teaspoon red wine vinegar
   Salt and freshly ground pepper

Preheat oven to 375°F or 400°F. Pierce eggplant, place on rack and bake until soft, about 50 to 60 minutes. Cool slightly, then split and scoop interior into large bowl and mash well. Mix in remaining ingredients, seasoning to taste with salt and pepper. Cover and chill until ready to serve.

Garbanzo-Sesame Spread

Makes about 2 cups

1 15½-ounce can garbanzo beans, drained
⅓ cup plus 2 tablespoons fresh lemon juice
¼ cup tahini (sesame paste)
3 tablespoons chopped green onion

2 garlic cloves
¼ teaspoon salt
Freshly ground pepper
Cilantro or parsley sprigs (garnish)
Toasted pita wedges

Puree first 7 ingredients in blender or processor. Transfer to bowl. Cover and refrigerate at least 30 minutes. Garnish with cilantro or parsley. Serve spread with toasted pita wedges.

Refritos

6 servings

1 16-ounce can red pinto or kidney beans, drained (reserve 1 tablespoon liquid)
Vegetable oil

1 finely minced garlic clove
Salt and freshly ground pepper
Homemade Taco Chips (see recipe, page 80)

Puree beans with liquid in blender or processor. Heat enough oil to cover bottom of pan and fry beans until slightly browned, stirring constantly. Mix in garlic. Season to taste with salt and pepper. Serve hot or at room temperature. Accompany with taco chips.

Festive Spinach Spread

Makes about 4 cups

2 10-ounce packages frozen chopped spinach, thawed, squeezed dry and pureed
1 cup sour cream
1 cup mayonnaise

1 7-ounce can sliced water chestnuts, drained
1 1⅝-ounce package imported dried vegetable soup mix
Cocktail rye rounds

Combine spinach, sour cream, mayonnaise, water chestnuts and soup mix in large bowl and blend thoroughly. Cover and refrigerate. Serve with rye rounds.

Mushroom Caviar

4 servings

3 tablespoons butter
½ pound mushrooms, wiped clean and finely chopped
4 shallots, minced
1 tablespoon dry white wine
1 garlic clove, minced

2 tablespoons toasted pine nuts
1 to 2 tablespoons sour cream
Salt and freshly ground pepper
Boston lettuce
Sesame crackers

Melt butter in large skillet over high heat. Add mushrooms and shallots and sauté, stirring frequently, about 5 minutes. Stir in wine and garlic and cook another minute. Remove from heat, transfer to bowl and let cool.

Gently mix in pine nuts and sour cream and season with salt and pepper. Cover and chill until ready to serve. Mound on lettuce leaves and accompany with sesame crackers.

Shrimp Spread

Makes about 2 cups

1 8-ounce package cream cheese, room temperature
1 7-ounce can tiny shrimp, rinsed and well drained
¼ cup mayonnaise
2 tablespoons fresh lemon juice

1 teaspoon chopped fresh parsley
½ teaspoon dried dillweed
½ teaspoon salt
 Thinly sliced black bread
 Crackers

Combine all but last 2 ingredients in mixing bowl and beat until well blended. Transfer to serving dish, cover and chill until ready to serve. Spread on black bread or crackers.

Vegetable Pâtés, Terrines and Mousses

Artichoke and Chestnut Pâté

Serve this pâté with thin whole wheat toast triangles or whole wheat crackers. Mango chutney and cumberland sauce are good accompaniments.

18 servings

1½ pounds chestnuts
6 bay leaves

1 7½-ounce can artichoke bottoms, drained (reserve ⅓ cup liquid)
3 slices whole wheat bread (crusts trimmed), cubed
3 eggs, beaten
½ cup finely chopped fresh parsley
⅓ cup sour cream

¼ cup finely chopped shallot
3 tablespoons unsalted butter (room temperature)
1 teaspoon herb or vegetable salt
½ teaspoon freshly grated nutmeg
⅛ teaspoon mace
½ cup coarsely chopped walnuts

 Watercress or parsley (garnish)

Make cut in side of each chestnut using small knife. Cook covered in boiling water with 2 bay leaves, 30 minutes. Remove outer shell and inner skin of each chestnut with small knife.

Preheat oven to 350°F. Chop chestnuts coarsely into about ¼-inch pieces. Transfer to large bowl of electric mixer. Chop artichoke bottoms coarsely into about ¼-inch pieces and add to chestnuts. Sprinkle bread cubes with reserved artichoke liquid and add to chestnuts. Add eggs, parsley, sour cream, shallot, butter, herb salt, nutmeg and mace and mix. Stir in chopped walnuts and beat well. Taste and adjust seasoning if necessary.

Coat 6-cup narrow nonmetal pâté mold or 10 × 4 × 3-inch loaf pan with vegetable oil (metal mold will discolor artichoke). Arrange remaining 4 bay leaves in bottom of pan. Press mixture into pan. Top with firm-fitting lid or cover top of mold tightly with waxed paper and then aluminum foil, crimping edges to make tight seal. Set mold in roasting pan. Pour in enough hot water to come halfway up sides of mold. Bake until set, about 1 hour. Discard wrapping; cover mold with waxed paper and weight with heavy object (a brick wrapped in aluminum foil works well). Refrigerate overnight.

Run sharp knife around edge of mold. Invert onto chilled serving platter. Garnish with watercress or parsley.

Pâté can be refrigerated for up to 1 week.

White Bean and Zucchini Pâté

6 to 8 servings

2 cups grated zucchini
Salt
3 tablespoons butter
1 small onion, chopped
1 garlic clove, pressed

3 cups cooked white beans
2 egg yolks

⅔ cup breadcrumbs made from firm-textured white bread
¼ cup whipping cream
3 tablespoons butter, melted

2 green onions, minced
2 tablespoons minced parsley
1½ teaspoons salt
¼ teaspoon coriander
¼ teaspoon thyme
¼ teaspoon chervil
¼ teaspoon basil
2 egg whites

2 tablespoons butter, melted
Tomato sauce, warmed (optional)

Preheat oven to 400°F. Butter 1½-quart loaf pan or charlotte mold.

Place zucchini in colander and sprinkle evenly with salt. Allow to drain 3 to 4 minutes, then squeeze gently to remove any remaining liquid. Melt 3 tablespoons butter in small skillet over medium-high heat. Add onion and sauté until transparent. Add garlic and sauté just until golden. Toss in zucchini and cook quickly 4 to 5 minutes, shaking pan or stirring constantly. Remove from heat and cool.

Puree beans in 2 batches in processor, adding 1 egg yolk to each batch, and transfer to large bowl; *or* puree through fine disc of food mill into large bowl and stir in both yolks.

Soak breadcrumbs in cream and stir into beans. Add 3 tablespoons melted butter, green onion, parsley, salt and herbs and mix well. Beat egg whites until stiff but not dry and fold into bean mixture.

Turn half of bean mixture into prepared pan or mold. Smooth top and spread zucchini mixture over in even layer. Spoon remaining bean mixture over zucchini and top with 2 tablespoons melted butter. Butter enough waxed paper to cover top of pan or mold; place buttered side down over pan and secure with twine. Set on rack in large pan with enough hot water to reach halfway up sides of pan or mold. Bake 45 minutes, or until top is golden. Remove from oven, discard waxed paper and let stand 20 minutes before unmolding. Slice and serve warm or cold. If served warm, spoon a small amount of tomato sauce on each slice.

Terrine of Garden Vegetables

A marvelous way to use leftover crudités. The Yogurt-Horseradish Sauce adds zest. Since few wines go well with horseradish, try a lusty one.

8 to 10 servings

½ pound green beans, trimmed

4 large carrots, trimmed

6 artichokes

1 head romaine

½ 10-ounce package frozen peas

Degreased chicken broth (homemade or commercial)

4 envelopes unflavored gelatin
Salt and freshly ground pepper
2 tablespoons prepared white horseradish

Yogurt-Horseradish Sauce (see following recipe)

Chill a 6-cup charlotte mold in freezer.

Cook green beans 7 minutes in covered saucepan in just enough unsalted boiling water to cover. Drain well, reserving cooking liquid. Transfer beans to small bowl, cover and refrigerate. Boil reserved cooking liquid over high heat until reduced to 2 tablespoons.

Cook carrots in covered saucepan in just enough unsalted water to cover until very tender. Drain well, reserving cooking liquid. Let carrots cool slightly, then chop coarsely. Transfer to separate bowl, cover and refrigerate. Boil cooking liquid over high heat until reduced to 2 tablespoons. Add to bean liquid.

Cook artichokes in boiling salted water until tender. Drain well. When cool enough to handle, remove leaves and chokes; reserve hearts for terrine. Transfer hearts to separate bowl and chill.

Wash romaine, discarding coarser ribs. Blanch dark green leaves 2 minutes. Drain well. When cool enough to handle, shred as for coleslaw. Refrigerate.

Cook peas in boiling water 3 minutes. Drain well. Transfer to separate bowl, cover and refrigerate.

Combine bean and carrot cooking liquids with enough chicken broth to measure 3 cups. Add gelatin and let stand 5 minutes to soften. Transfer to small saucepan and heat gently, stirring until gelatin is dissolved. Remove from heat, taste and season with salt, pepper and horseradish, blending well. Remove mold from freezer and quickly swirl several tablespoons of gelatin mixture around sides and bottom (it should set almost immediately).

Crisscross a few green beans on bottom of mold to make a lattice pattern. Stand a few more beans upright around edge (longer ones will be trimmed later).

Layer carrots evenly over latticed beans. Top with peas. Arrange remaining beans over peas. Top with shredded romaine. Place 1 artichoke heart in center of mold and surround with remaining 5. Slowly add remaining gelatin to mold. Refrigerate until set.

When set, trim any beans extending over mold. To serve, dip terrine briefly into pan of hot water and invert onto platter. Cut into wedges and serve with Yogurt-Horseradish Sauce.

Yogurt-Horseradish Sauce

Makes about 1½ cups

1 cup plain yogurt
½ cup mayonnaise
2 tablespoons prepared white horseradish or to taste

Blend all ingredients. Cover and chill.

Carrot and Spinach Striped Pâté

18 servings

½ cup water
2 tablespoons light vegetable oil (preferably cold-pressed safflower)
¼ cup unflavored gelatin
¼ cup whole wheat pastry flour
1 cup milk or reconstituted nonfat dry milk

Carrot Mixture
4 cups sliced carrot
1 tablespoon light vegetable oil (preferably cold-pressed safflower)
½ cup chopped yellow onion
½ teaspoon finely chopped garlic
2 tablespoons tomato paste
2 teaspoons curry powder
½ teaspoon meat flavoring
½ teaspoon dry mustard
¼ teaspoon freshly grated nutmeg
Herb or vegetable salt
½ cup pistachio nuts, blanched in salted water and drained

Spinach Mixture
2 pounds fresh spinach, well washed (do not remove stems)
1 tablespoon light vegetable oil (preferably cold-pressed safflower)
½ cup chopped yellow onion
1 teaspoon finely chopped garlic
8 ounces mushrooms, coarsely chopped
1 teaspoon fresh lemon juice
1 teaspoon ground cardamom
1 teaspoon finely chopped fresh tarragon or ½ teaspoon dried, crumbled
1 teaspoon finely chopped fresh chervil or 1 tablespoon finely chopped fresh parsley
Herb or vegetable salt

2 cups Tomato-Herb Aspic (see following recipe)
Watercress or parsley (garnish)
Crisped carrot curls (garnish)

Bring water and oil to boil over medium heat in small saucepan. Remove from heat. Combine gelatin and flour in small bowl. Add to water and stir until smooth. Blend in milk. Return to heat and stir until mixture comes to boil and thickens. Freeze until just set, about 7 to 10 minutes.

For carrot mixture: Preheat oven to 325°F. Cook sliced carrot in boiling water until crisp-tender. Drain and set aside. Heat 1 tablespoon vegetable oil in large skillet over medium heat. Add onion and garlic and cook until onion is translucent. Reduce heat to low, add tomato paste, curry powder and meat flavoring and cook, stirring constantly, 2 minutes. Transfer to food processor. Add carrot and puree until smooth (or press through fine strainer into bowl). Add ⅓ of gelatin mixture with mustard, nutmeg and herb salt to taste and mix well. Fold in pistachio nuts.

For spinach mixture: Place spinach in large saucepan and sprinkle with water. Cover and cook over medium-high heat, stirring occasionally, until wilted, about 2 to 3 minutes. Drain spinach in colander. Place between paper towels and squeeze dry. Transfer to processor and puree until smooth. Heat 1 tablespoon vegetable oil in small skillet over medium heat. Add onion and garlic and cook until onion is translucent. Increase heat to high, add mushrooms and lemon juice and cook 2 minutes. Add to spinach with remaining gelatin mixture, cardamom, tarragon and chervil and puree again. Season with herb salt to taste. (If not using processor, press spinach, onion and mushroom mixture through fine grinder and combine with other ingredients in large bowl of electric mixer.)

Coat 2-quart pâté mold or 9 × 5-inch loaf pan with oil. Spread half of spinach mixture on bottom. Carefully spread all of carrot mixture over spinach. Top with remaining spinach mixture. Cover top of mold tightly with waxed paper and then aluminum foil, crimping edges to make tight seal. Set mold in roasting pan. Pour enough hot water into pan to come halfway up sides of mold. Bake until set, about 2 hours. Remove mold from pan but do not unwrap. Weight with heavy object (a brick wrapped in aluminum foil works well). Let cool to room temperature. Refrigerate at least 12 hours.

Invert pâté onto chilled serving platter. Coarsely chop aspic and spoon in border around pâté. Garnish with watercress sprigs and carrot curls.

Pâté can be refrigerated up to 1 week.

Tomato-Herb Aspic
_____

Makes about 2 cups

3 egg whites
2¼ cups vegetable or chicken stock
2 tablespoons unflavored gelatin
1 tablespoon tomato paste

½ teaspoon dried tarragon or thyme, crumbled

Beat egg whites in large bowl until soft peaks form. Add stock, gelatin, tomato paste and tarragon and mix well. Pour mixture into tin-lined copper or heavy enameled saucepan. Whisk over medium heat until boiling. Remove from heat and let stand 15 minutes; do not stir. Line large strainer or colander with damp cloth and place over large bowl. Pour mixture through strainer. Transfer to 8 × 8 × 2-inch nonstick cake pan. Chill until set, about 2 hours.

Avocado and Radish Mousse with Radish Pompons

12 to 14 servings

2 ripe avocados (7 to 8 ounces each)
½ cup mayonnaise
3 tablespoons fresh lemon juice
½ teaspoon sea salt or 1 teaspoon coarse salt
 Ground red pepper

¼ cup plus 2 tablespoons water
3 tablespoons unflavored gelatin

1 cup shredded red radishes
4 egg whites

4 to 6 medium whole red radishes (garnish)

4 to 6 watercress sprigs (garnish)

Oil 1½-quart ring mold (or six 6- to 8-ounce ramekins). Invert on paper towels and set aside to drain.

Peel and halve avocados. Transfer to processor and puree. Add mayonnaise, 2 tablespoons lemon juice, salt and pepper and mix well. Set aside.

Combine water, gelatin and 1 tablespoon lemon juice in small saucepan and cook over medium heat, stirring constantly, until gelatin is dissolved. Remove from heat and let cool slightly. Add gelatin mixture to avocado a little at a time, beating constantly.

Pat shredded radishes dry between paper towels and set aside. Beat egg whites in large bowl until soft peaks form. Carefully fold avocado mixture into egg whites. Stir in shredded radishes. Fill mold(s) with mousse. Refrigerate at least 8 hours or overnight.

For radish pompons: Cut root and stem from each radish. Thinly slice each radish lengthwise from root end *almost* through to stem end. Slice again at opposite angle from root end *almost* through to stem end. Transfer radishes to bowl of ice and refrigerate.

Before serving, pat pompons dry with paper towels. Set mousse in bowl of hot water briefly to loosen. Slide small thin knife around inside edges of mold(s) and invert mold(s) onto serving platter. Garnish mousse with radish pompons and watercress sprigs.

🍓 Pâté Primer

General Tips

1. Rectangular terrines or loaf pans are the most practical because slices are easier to remove. Oval terrines are lovely, but contents should be unmolded before slicing.

2. Pâtés are best cooked slowly, never more than 350°F, in a bain-marie. This cuts down on shrinkage and keeps the fat where it belongs—in the pâté. Meat pâtés are done when they register 160°F on a meat thermometer inserted into the middle. You will know that your custard-based and fish pâtés are done when a metal larding needle inserted into the middle comes out clean.

3. Seasoning *must* be checked by cooking and tasting a small amount of the basic pâté mixture in advance. It should be quite spicy since cold foods taste bland unless they are slightly overseasoned.

4. Don't place a weight on a pâté; it only serves to squeeze out the flavorful meat juices and the tenderizing fat. Give a cooked pâté a night in the refrigerator so flavors can blend and juices congeal.

5. If aspic is desired, you may use this shortcut: Take a can of beef bouillon, perk up the flavor with a few tablespoons of Cognac and a few grindings of pepper, and add one tablespoon unflavored gelatin per cup and a half of liquid. When the pâté is cooked but still hot, drain off the floating fat and fill to the top with aspic. Refrigerate as usual.

6. Meat terrines do not take well to freezing, so when you have too much left over, just crumble into a saucepan with oregano and tomato sauce and let simmer an hour or so. You will have divine spaghetti sauce! Or try frying a sliced meat pâté and serving as you would sausage.

Basic Proportions

Meat Pâtés
A good general basic forcemeat:

⅓ **pound finely ground lean veal**
⅓ **pound finely ground lean pork, shoulder preferred**

⅓ **pound coarsely ground fresh pork back fat**

Note the ⅓ fat proportion. To this add 1 egg, ¾ teaspoon salt, ¾ teaspoon of any combination of ground pepper, bay leaves, cloves, nutmeg, thyme, oregano, sage, savory or basil, plus appropriate spirits and citrus peel.

Forcemeat is what eggs are to a soufflé—the basic fabric. To it you may add diced or julienne of ham, tongue, veal, chicken, rabbit, duck, game, nuts, fruits. The trick is to anticipate whether these agents are going to *add* or *absorb* moisture. Raw meats and nuts absorb moisture from the basic forcemeat. Weigh the quantity you intend to use and to the forcemeat add fat equal to one-half the weight of the additional meats and/or nuts. This maintains the one-third fat balance. Cooked or cured meats, such as ham and tongue, don't require rebalancing.

When fruits or vegetables are used in a meat pâté, they are inclined to give off moisture. To facilitate slicing, add to the forcemeat one tablespoon of flour per half cup of fruit or vegetables called for.

When making a rabbit, pheasant or poultry pâté, it is often desirable to reinforce the flavor by adding to the forcemeat ½ cup of rich, condensed stock made from the bones. This is worth the extra time and effort.

Fish Pâtés

The basic proportion is one egg white and one cup of heavy cream per pound of raw fish, seasoned to taste. The seafoods most often used for fish terrines are shrimp, salmon, pike, sole, lobster and scallops because they contain large amounts of natural gelatin and do not exude their juices in cooking. Other fish can be used but must be helped along by the inclusion either of a *panade* (you can use one cup of a basic four-egg cream puff recipe) or a good handful of sea scallops ground along with the fish—either of which tends to stabilize a flaky fish without noticeably changing its taste.

In the bowl of a food processor, puree fish, egg white and seasoning. Drizzle in cream, which should be very cold, and once the cream has been absorbed, do not continue to process. This just whips the cream.

Fish pâtés take well to decoration with morsels of fish, vegetables or chopped herbs. Be sure that there is fish mousse between the decorative elements, like mortar between bricks, and that any vegetables are properly cooked, drained and dried.

Vegetable Pâtés

These *méchants enfants* of the nouvelle cuisine tend to fall into two categories: those bound with gelatin and those bound in a rather stiff custard. With both, however, the vegetables must be thoroughly cooked and drained prior to assembly. Almost any vegetables will do in a vegetable terrine, but beets should be avoided as they dye everything red, and celery has strings that are impossible to cut through.

When using gelatin, four tablespoons of gelatin to three cups of liquid will yield a firm, shiny terrine that can be thinly sliced. Somehow the quantity of gelatin is not objectionable as long as the accompanying sauce possesses sufficient character to distract from the texture.

When making custard-based vegetable pâté, the creamy consistency of a dessert is undesirable. The pâté must be firm enough to be sliced. A good base is one cup ham or white meat of chicken, half an onion, three eggs, one cup of milk, and seasonings, all pureed in the processor. Butter a small (four-cup) terrine, line the bottom with waxed paper and alternate layers of custard and vegetables. Bake covered in a bainmarie for approximately one hour at 350°F; chill and unmold.

Seafood Pâtés, Terrines and Mousses

Shrimp Pâté

2 servings

¼ pound cooked baby shrimp
1 small garlic clove
2 tablespoons (¼ stick) unsalted butter

4 teaspoons whipping cream
1 teaspoon dry Sherry
Salt and freshly ground pepper
¼ teaspoon dried dillweed

Combine first 5 ingredients with salt and pepper in processor or blender and mix until smooth. Stir in dillweed. Spoon into small ramekin and sprinkle with additional dillweed. Serve chilled or at room temperature.

Terrine of Leeks, Truffles and Fillet of Sole

There are those who swear they can taste the sea and truffles in the dry white wines from Graves. Enjoy your truffles in this terrine and let the wine provide its counterpoint.

8 to 10 servings

6 medium leeks, trimmed of roots and dark green ends

2 truffles (cut 5 or 6 thin slices and coarsely chop remainder)

1 pound fillet of sole
½ pound sea scallops
2 egg whites

2 teaspoons salt
1½ teaspoons freshly ground white pepper
¼ teaspoon freshly grated nutmeg
1½ cups well-chilled whipping cream

Fresh Tomato Sauce (see following recipe)

Halve leeks lengthwise. Wash well to remove sand and grit. Boil 10 minutes in salted water; drain well.

Generously butter 5-cup terrine. Arrange a row of truffle slices down the center. Using prettiest ribbons of leek, line entire terrine, placing leeks from center out to edge and extending beyond pan all the way around terrine. Finely chop remaining leeks.

Preheat oven to 325°F. Combine sole, scallops, egg whites, salt, pepper and nutmeg in processor and grind finely. With machine running, add cream in thin stream until it is thoroughly absorbed and mixture is sticky. Quickly mix in chopped leeks using on/off turns.

Pack ⅓ of fish mixture into terrine, being careful not to disturb leeks or truffle slices. Sprinkle with half of chopped truffles. Layer with another ⅓ of fish mixture and sprinkle with remaining truffles. Cover with remaining fish mixture. Fold leek ends over to enclose fish mixture. Cover with foil. Place in shallow pan filled with hot water. Bake until set, about 1 hour. Cool slightly, then refrigerate overnight. Invert onto serving platter. Slice with very sharp knife, being sure to cut completely through. Serve with sauce.

Fresh Tomato Sauce

8 ripe large tomatoes
⅓ cup finely snipped chives
2 tablespoons olive oil

1 tablespoon tomato paste
Salt and freshly ground pepper

Blanch tomatoes in boiling water until skins split, about 1 minute. Transfer to colander and run under cold water until cool to the touch. Peel and seed. Pass pulp through fine strainer into mixing bowl. (If tomatoes are watery or not as flavorful as they could be, reduce over medium-high heat to concentrate flavor, stirring constantly.) Add remaining ingredients and blend well.

Sole, Salmon and Scallop Mousse with Sauce Verte

25 servings

2 pounds fillet of sole, pureed and thoroughly chilled
2¼ cups whipping cream
2 egg whites
1½ teaspoons salt
½ teaspoon freshly ground white pepper
½ teaspoon freshly grated nutmeg

2 pounds fillet of salmon (reserve 4 slices 3 × 8 × ⅛ inches), pureed, thoroughly chilled
1¾ cups whipping cream
2 egg whites
1 teaspoon salt
¾ teaspoon ground red pepper
¾ teaspoon freshly grated nutmeg

1½ pounds scallops (reserve 18), pureed, thoroughly chilled
2¼ cups whipping cream
1½ teaspoons salt
½ teaspoon freshly ground white pepper

½ teaspoon freshly grated nutmeg
2 bunches spinach, washed, stemmed and blanched

Sauce Verte
1 cup mayonnaise (preferably homemade)
½ cup loosely packed fresh parsley leaves
½ cup loosely packed watercress leaves
1 tablespoon fresh lemon juice
2½ teaspoons capers, rinsed and drained
1½ teaspoons dried tarragon, crumbled
¾ teaspoon Worcestershire sauce
¼ teaspoon granulated garlic
Dash of hot pepper sauce
1½ cups whipping cream
Salt and freshly ground pepper

Transfer chilled sole to stainless steel bowl and set in larger bowl filled with ice. Whisking constantly, gradually add whipping cream in slow, steady stream until well blended. Beat egg whites in medium bowl until frothy; fold into fish mixture. Season with salt, pepper and nutmeg. Cook 2 spoonfuls sole mixture in small skillet over medium heat until opaque. Taste and adjust seasoning for uncooked mixture as necessary. Repeat procedure in separate bowls with salmon and scallops. Refrigerate thoroughly.

Preheat oven to 300°F. Line two 9 × 5-inch loaf pans with oiled parchment paper. Divide sole mousse between prepared pans, smoothing carefully with spatula. Arrange 1 slice of reserved salmon over top of each. Cover each with layer of 3 to 4 large spinach leaves. Divide salmon mousse into fourths. Spread ¼ of salmon mousse over spinach leaves in *each* pan, smoothing carefully.

Spread out 5 to 6 large spinach leaves on work surface with long ends overlapping slightly. Arrange 9 reserved whole scallops down center. Carefully roll leaves into cylinders, covering scallops completely. Using spatula, transfer to center of 1 loaf pan. Repeat with remaining reserved scallops for other pan. Spread another ¼ of salmon mousse in *each* pan, smoothing top.

Cover salmon mousse with single layer of spinach leaves. Cover each with another salmon slice (molds should be ⅔ full). Fill to top with scallop mousse.

Cover pans with oiled parchment paper and set in large shallow pan. Add enough boiling water to come halfway up sides of loaf pans.

Bake until mousse is set and thermometer inserted in center registers 120°F, about 1 to 1¼ hours. Let stand at room temperature until cool. Place light weight over top of each mousse and refrigerate overnight.

For sauce: Combine first 9 ingredients in processor or blender and mix well. Add cream and mix until thickened. Season with salt and pepper to taste.

To serve, run sharp knife around edges of molds, dip molds briefly into hot water and invert mousse onto platter. Carefully remove parchment paper and discard. Slice mousse using damp sharp knife. Serve with Sauce Verte.

🍏 Caviar

Experts agree that size and color of caviar have nothing to do with quality and flavor. The only acceptable test is the palate. The large-size, light gray eggs, favored by the American marketplace, are produced by beluga sturgeon. In Europe the general preference runs to the smaller grained sweeter gray sevruga. The connoisseur's caviar, however, is the nutty osietra, with its eggs casting a gold-green light.

Unfortunately, even the most ardent devotee may never have the opportunity to taste the rarest of all caviar, the golden roe of the sterlet sturgeon, said to be discreetly sent to the Kremlin. Only about 40 pounds of sterlet is produced annually. In earlier times when production was more plentiful, about 100 pounds a year, legend has it that the precious sterlet caviar was wrapped in sable and rushed to the Imperial Palace in St. Petersburg.

No doubt a certain mystique adheres to tasting and affording the finest caviars today. One man we know came by a tin of golden sterlet caviar, but only through a friend in Paris who had a connection in the Kremlin. He describes the taste of sterlet caviar as "velvety and smooth, dry and wonderful," eaten *au naturel,* of course, with possibly a drop of lemon, freshly squeezed from a wedge, and a dash of ground pepper.

We can envy the mortal whose lips embraced the rare and elusive sterlet. For him, dipping a silver spoon into that chilled bowl of perfection was running the bulls in Pamplona or a solo sailing of the Atlantic or seeing the snow leopard in Tibet. A triumph.

Buying and Serving

The sturgeons: Fresh beluga and osietra caviars are priced at several hundred dollars per pound. Sevruga costs about half their price. Pajusnaya, the pressed product from any of these varieties, is the best buy. Fresh Iranian caviar is available in the original two-kilo tins (about five pounds) and in smaller amounts, repackaged from the original tins. Vacuum packed pasteurized caviar is available in sizes starting with one ounce.

Caviar Mousse

8 to 12 appetizer servings

4 ounces red lumpfish caviar
3 tablespoons chopped fresh parsley
2 tablespoons finely minced Spanish onion
1 cup sour cream

¼ teaspoon freshly ground pepper
1½ teaspoons unflavored gelatin
2 tablespoons water
½ cup whipping cream, whipped
Cucumber slices
Rye melba toast

Set aside 2 tablespoons caviar, 1 tablespoon parsley and 1 tablespoon onion for garnish; cover and refrigerate. Combine remaining caviar, parsley and onion with sour cream and pepper in medium-size nonmetallic bowl and blend well. Sprinkle gelatin over water in small saucepan. Stir over low heat until gelatin dissolves completely. Remove from heat and stir into caviar mixture. Fold in whipped cream. Turn into 2-cup nonmetal crock or mold. Cover and refrigerate until set. Let stand at room temperature 15 minutes before serving. Spoon mousse from crock or unmold onto nonmetal platter. Surround with cucumber slices and melba toast. Garnish top with reserved caviar, parsley and onion.

When purchasing the whole two-kilo tin, don't be afraid to request that the shopkeeper open the container for your inspection. The tin should be filled to capacity, eggs bright and firm. Too much moisture would suggest that the eggs have been crushed by poor handling. Can you ask for a taste? That depends on your relationship with the store owner.

Enjoying fresh caviar can be a simple matter of placing a spoonful on the back of the hand between thumb and index finger and imbibing the precious substance unaccompanied. That, we are told, is the way of the ultimate connoisseur. Simplest is indeed best when dealing with fine, sweet caviar; serve it chilled and mounded over toast, fresh bread, plain crackers or cucumber rounds. Or spread a little sweet butter first, then add caviar and a drop of lemon juice. A garniture of chopped hard-cooked egg and chopped onion lends an elegant note.

The Russian Tea Room in Manhattan serves caviar with blini, small round buckwheat crepes: one spoonful caviar, one spoonful sweet butter, roll in a crepe and down with icy vodka.

The affordables: The roe of the lumpfish from the Arctic sea, the whitefish from North American waters and salmon from Alaska are reasonably priced and widely available in vacuum-packed two- to eight-ounce jars.

The "affordables" may be served in the classic ways just like their Caspian cousins. They lend themselves, further, to a whole range of inspirations: Blended with cream cheese, caviar makes a handsome stuffing for avocados, mushrooms or celery; or combined with Swiss cheese, a handsome caviar quiche; it's a wonderful last-minute addition to potato salad; or try a caviar pie to which cream cheese, sour cream and chopped egg have been added.

Unopened, a container of fresh caviar may be kept in the refrigerator for up to six weeks. Once opened, all caviar, fresh or vacuum packed, is highly perishable. Keep refrigerated and use within two weeks.

Caviar Ring

4 to 6 servings

1 teaspoon unflavored gelatin
2 tablespoons dry Sherry
2 tablespoons fresh lemon juice

6 hard-cooked eggs
1 cup mayonnaise
1 teaspoon anchovy paste

1 teaspoon Worcestershire sauce
1 2½-ounce jar lumpfish caviar
Parsley sprigs (garnish)
Sesame rice crackers or black bread

Generously grease 2-cup mold. Soften gelatin in Sherry and lemon juice in small heatproof container about 5 minutes, then place over very low heat until dissolved, stirring several times.

Chop eggs in processor or blender. Transfer to mixing bowl. Stir in gelatin mixture, mayonnaise, anchovy paste and Worcestershire and mix thoroughly. Gently fold in caviar until well blended. Turn into mold, cover and refrigerate until firm. Unmold and garnish with parsley sprigs. Surround with crackers or thin slices of black bread.

Striped Bass Mold with Vegetable Floral Design

Serve with toasted bread thins.

12 servings

2 cups Fish Aspic (see following recipe)

1 pound striped bass fillets
1 cup white wine

3 tablespoons butter
3 tablespoons all purpose flour
¾ cup fish stock or clam juice
2 tablespoons fresh lemon juice

1 cup Fish Aspic (see following recipe)
¾ cup whipping cream, whipped
¼ pound Nova Scotia salmon, cut into 1 × ¼-inch strips
Salt and freshly ground white pepper

3 thin slices carrot, cut into 5-pointed stars
3 pieces black olive, trimmed into ¼-inch rounds
3 small celery leaf sprigs or parsley leaves

Geranium or poinsettia blooms (optional garnish)

Pour 2 cups Fish Aspic into shallow pan (aspic should be about ¼ inch deep). Set aside in refrigerator to firm.

Generously oil 6-cup charlotte mold or other deep mold and set aside. Rinse fish in cool water and pat dry with paper towels. Combine fish and wine in large saucepan over high heat and bring to boil. Reduce heat to low, cover and cook fish until just opaque, about 5 to 7 minutes (do not overcook). Drain fish well. Transfer to processor and mix to thick paste. Transfer to large mixing bowl.

Melt butter in small saucepan over medium heat. Reduce heat to low, add flour and whisk 2 minutes. Slowly add fish stock or clam juice and lemon juice, whisking until sauce is thick and smooth, about 3 to 5 minutes. Let cool.

Stir sauce into fish. Add ¾ cup Fish Aspic and mix well. Gently fold in whipped cream, salmon strips and salt and pepper. Turn mixture into mold. Chill. *(Can be prepared 1 to 2 days ahead to this point, covered and refrigerated.)*

For floral bouquet pattern: Arrange carrot stars on small saucer no larger than top of charlotte mold. Place olive pieces in centers of carrot (to resemble flower). Use celery or parsley for stems and leaves. Spoon ¼ cup Fish Aspic over and around vegetable pattern. Refrigerate until firm.

To assemble: Run sharp knife around inside edge of mold. Place hot towel briefly on bottom and invert mold onto serving platter. Set saucer holding floral arrangement on warm towel just until barely loosened. Tip saucer carefully and slide decoration into place on top of mold. Chop remaining aspic into ½-inch dice and arrange around base of mold. Decorate with geraniums or poinsettia blooms.

Fish Aspic

Makes 3 cups

2 egg whites
3 cups fish stock
2 crushed egg shells

⅓ cup cool water
1½ tablespoons unflavored gelatin

Beat egg whites in medium bowl until soft peaks form. Transfer to 1½- to 2-quart saucepan. Add 3 cups fish stock and crushed egg shells.

Mix water and gelatin in small bowl until gelatin is dissolved. Add gelatin mixture to fish stock. Place over medium-high heat and bring to boil, stirring frequently. Reduce heat immediately and simmer without stirring until crust forms on top and liquid below is clear, about 15 to 20 minutes. Carefully pour mixture into medium bowl through strainer lined with double thickness of cheesecloth.

Shrimp Mousse with Avocado Surprise

There is something about this mousse that suggests serving tequila—either straight or mixed as a Margarita. But a crisp, young rosé would be equally appropriate. Be sure to invite enough guests to enjoy this terrine the first time around, since the avocado tends to darken slightly upon standing.

8 servings

¾ **pound shelled uncooked shrimp (1 pound before shelling)**
1 **egg white**
1 **tablespoon tomato paste**
1 **large garlic clove**
2 **teaspoons salt**
  Pinch of ground red pepper

1½ **cups well-chilled whipping cream**
  Juice of 1 lemon
2 **envelopes unflavored gelatin**
1 **ripe avocado**
  Salt and freshly ground white pepper

Preheat oven to 350°F. Oil 4-cup terrine. Cut piece of waxed paper to fit bottom of terrine. Set in terrine; lightly oil top of paper.

Combine shrimp, egg white, tomato paste, garlic, salt and ground red pepper in processor and puree. With machine running, add cream in thin stream and mix until smooth and sticky. Transfer to bowl, cover and refrigerate.

Squeeze lemon juice into measuring cup or dish. Add enough water to measure ½ cup. Add gelatin and let stand to soften. Set cup in pan of gently simmering water and stir until gelatin is dissolved. Peel and seed avocado and puree in processor. Add gelatin, salt and white pepper and blend well.

To assemble: Spread about ⅔ of shrimp mousse evenly over bottom and sides of terrine. Spoon avocado puree into center. Cover with remaining mousse, making sure no avocado shows through the top (avocado puree must be completely enclosed or it will discolor).

Cover terrine with foil. Place in shallow pan of hot water and bake until set, about 45 minutes. Cool slightly, then refrigerate overnight before serving.

🍎 *Poultry and Meat Pâtés and Terrines*

Chicken and Hazelnut Terrine

Warm saké is our choice of spirits here. It heightens and plays on the flavors of this rich terrine. For the less adventuresome, a fine Meursault from the Côte de Beaune provides good balance.

8 to 10 servings

  Thinly sliced barding fat
2 **quarts (8 cups) rich homemade chicken stock**
1 **pound chicken meat (dark and light combined)**
¾ **pound fresh pork back fat**
2 **eggs**

1 **tablespoon all purpose flour**
1½ **teaspoons salt**
1 **teaspoon freshly ground white pepper**
¼ **cup whipping cream**
¼ **pound whole hazelnuts, toasted**

Line 5-cup terrine with barding fat. Boil stock in large saucepan over high heat until reduced to 1 cup. Remove from heat and cool completely. Taste; if stock is salty, omit salt from recipe.

Cut ¼ pound chicken into small cubes and set aside. Preheat oven to 350°F.

Combine remaining chicken with pork back fat in processor and chop coarsely using on/off turns; *do not grind too finely.* Transfer ¾ of mixture to large bowl. To remaining mixture add eggs, flour, salt and pepper and process until creamy. Add to chopped mixture.

Blend in cream, hazelnuts, cubed chicken and stock. Pack into terrine. Cover with foil. Place in large, shallow pan. Pour enough boiling water into pan to come halfway up sides of terrine. Bake until set, about 1½ hours (remove foil during last half hour to brown top, if desired). Cool slightly; refrigerate overnight.

Country Pâté with Bacon

Should be made at least two days ahead and refrigerated to mellow.

12 servings

1 pound chicken livers, trimmed
½ cup fresh orange juice
1 cup dried mushrooms (1 ounce), finely chopped
½ cup dry Sherry

8 small (or 6 medium) garlic cloves, quartered
3 eggs
½ cup brandy or Cognac
¼ cup whipping cream
1 tablespoon salt
2 teaspoons freshly ground white pepper
1 teaspoon allspice

1 pound veal, 1 pound pork shoulder and ¾ pound pork fat (from fresh ham or pork loin), ground together
½ cup all purpose flour
½ cup shelled pistachio nuts (about 3 ounces)
1 large black truffle, finely diced (optional)

1 pound sliced bacon

Bay leaves or fresh parsley sprigs (garnish)

Combine chicken livers and orange juice in medium bowl. Mix mushrooms with Sherry in small bowl. Let both mixtures marinate 30 minutes (stir mushrooms occasionally).

Combine garlic, eggs, brandy, cream, salt, pepper and allspice in another bowl and blend lightly.

Drain livers well. Add to garlic mixture. Add half to processor or blender and mix until smooth. Pour into large mixing bowl. Repeat with remaining liver mixture. Stir in ground meats. Sift flour over mixture and blend well. Mix in nuts, truffle and drained mushrooms and set aside.

Preheat oven to 400°F. Overlap 4 slices of bacon to form cross in bottom of 10 × 4-inch round baking dish, allowing 1- to 2-inch overhang. Fill in empty spaces with shorter bacon slices. Pour in liver mixture to within 1 inch of top. Tap dish lightly against counter to remove air bubbles. Fold overhanging ends of bacon over liver mixture. Cover dish with foil and set in shallow baking pan. Add enough boiling water to pan to come halfway up sides of dish. Bake until set, about 3 hours, adding more water to pan as necessary and removing foil during last 15 minutes to brown top. Remove from oven and re-cover with foil. Weight pâté with heavy object (a similar size pan with foil-wrapped brick in center works well). Refrigerate. *(Can be made ahead and refrigerated 7 to 10 days.)*

Serve in baking dish or immerse briefly in hot water and unmold onto serving platter. Discard any remaining bacon fat. Garnish with bay leaves or parsley.

Artichoke Bottoms with Pâté

6 to 8 servings

1 14-ounce can artichoke bottoms

1 tablespoon butter or margarine
½ pound fresh chicken livers
1 finely chopped small onion
Pinch of thyme

4 mushrooms, coarsely chopped

1 tablespoon brandy

Salt and freshly ground pepper
1 hard-cooked egg yolk, sieved (garnish)

Drain artichoke bottoms and reserve juice. Set aside.

Melt butter in skillet over low heat; add livers, onion, thyme and mushrooms; sauté about 8 minutes. Livers should be pink inside.

Heat brandy and ignite. Pour over livers. Transfer contents of skillet to blender or processor and whirl until smooth. Cool in refrigerator.

Season with salt and pepper to taste. Spoon a generous amount of pâté on top of each artichoke bottom and garnish with sieved egg. Serve cold.

Duck Liver Pâté in Port Aspic

This pâté is equally delicious prepared with chicken livers. Prepare two loaves to serve 25 guests.

12 servings

Port Aspic
2 teaspoons unflavored gelatin
1 cup Port

2 tablespoons sugar
1 tablespoon water
3 tablespoons red wine vinegar
½ teaspoon dried tarragon, crumbled

Duck Liver Pâté
1 pound duck (or chicken) livers
1 cup milk

¼ cup Cognac

1¼ cups (2½ sticks) butter, room temperature
1 cup sliced onion
1 small green apple, peeled, cored and sliced

¼ cup Sherry or applejack
¼ cup whipping cream

1¼ teaspoons salt
1 teaspoon fresh lemon juice

For aspic: Generously butter 8 × 4-inch loaf pan and set aside. Dissolve gelatin in small bowl with ¼ cup Port.

Meanwhile, combine sugar and water in medium saucepan over medium-high heat, stirring until dissolved. Cook until mixture is dark caramel color, about 8 to 10 minutes. Whisk in vinegar, remaining Port and tarragon. Reduce heat and simmer about 2 minutes. Add gelatin, stirring until dissolved. Strain aspic through cheesecloth-lined colander into prepared loaf pan, covering ⅛ to ¼ inch of bottom. Chill until set.

For pâté: Combine the duck livers, milk and Cognac in medium bowl and soak 1 hour.

Melt ½ cup butter in large skillet over medium heat. Add onion and sauté until browned. Add apple and cook until softened, about 3 to 4 minutes. Transfer mixture to processor or blender using slotted spoon.

Drain livers. Return skillet to medium-high heat. Add livers and sauté until just pink, about 10 to 12 minutes. Add to onion mixture in processor or blender. Reduce heat to medium, add Sherry to skillet and cook, stirring up any browned bits clinging to bottom of pan. Add pan juices and ¼ cup cream to liver mixture and puree until smooth. Let stand until lukewarm.

Beat remaining butter in medium bowl until creamy. With machine running, gradually blend butter into liver mixture. Mix in salt and lemon juice. Pour over chilled aspic, smoothing top. Refrigerate. To serve, run sharp knife around edge of mold, dip mold briefly into hot water and invert pâté onto platter.

Ham and Fennel Seed Terrine

A cornucopia of pleasures for all the senses. Pernod, fennel-flavored Aquavit or Anisette works well as an accompaniment. Or serve a young Chablis.

8 to 10 servings

Thinly sliced barding fat
½ pound coarsely ground veal
½ pound coarsely ground pork
½ pound fresh pork back fat, coarsely ground
2 eggs
2 tablespoons Pernod
1 heaping tablespoon fennel seed

2 teaspoons salt
2 teaspoons Spice Parisienne (see following recipe)
½ pound Virginia ham, cut into long "chopstick" strips
⅓ cup shelled pistachio nuts, skinned

Line 5-cup terrine with barding fat. Combine all remaining ingredients except ham and nuts in large bowl and mix with whipping motion to aerate. Spread about ¼ to ⅓ of mixture in terrine. Arrange some strips of ham lengthwise on top and sprinkle with some of nuts. Repeat layering, ending with veal mixture. Cover with foil and refrigerate overnight (this will assure a lovely pink color as the ham will cure with the surrounding veal mixture).

Preheat oven to 350°F. Place terrine in large, shallow pan. Pour enough boiling water into pan to come halfway up sides of terrine. Bake until meat thermometer inserted into center registers 160°F, about 1½ to 2 hours. Cool slightly, then refrigerate 1 to 2 days.

Spice Parisienne

Makes about ¼ cup

2 teaspoons ground coriander
2 teaspoons dried tarragon, finely crushed
2 teaspoons ground allspice
1 teaspoon freshly grated nutmeg

1 teaspoon ground cinnamon
½ teaspoon ground cardamom
½ teaspoon dried marjoram, finely crushed
⅛ teaspoon ground cloves

Combine all spices in tightly covered jar. It is not necessary to refrigerate.

Pork Terrine with Prunes

Prunes and Armagnac have a natural affinity, and you may wish to try this with the fine brandy of Gascony. But since this is a trencherman's terrine made for lusty eating and crusty breads, beer in frosted glasses seems just right.

8 servings

Thinly sliced barding fat
⅓ pound ground pork
⅓ pound ground veal
⅓ pound ground fresh pork back fat
¼ pound diced uncooked pork or ham
1 egg
1 tablespoon all purpose flour

1½ teaspoons salt
1½ teaspoons Spice Parisienne (see preceding recipe)
¼ teaspoon freshly grated nutmeg
12 dried pitted prunes, coarsely chopped
½ cup Port

Preheat oven to 350°F. Line 4-cup terrine with barding fat. Thoroughly combine remaining ingredients except prunes and Port in large mixing bowl. Add prunes and Port and mix gently.

Pack into prepared terrine. Cover with foil. Place in large, shallow pan. Pour enough boiling water into pan to come halfway up sides of terrine. Bake until meat thermometer inserted into center of terrine registers 160°F, about 1½ to 2 hours (remove foil during last half hour of baking to brown, if desired). Cool slightly, then refrigerate overnight before slicing and serving.

Clockwise from top left: Eggplant with Prosciutto and Bel Paese, Spinach Timbales with Fonduta, Grilled Mushrooms with Marrow and Herbs, Angel of Death Cheese

*Clockwise from top: Raw Radish Sauce with crudités, Avocado
Gazpacho Mold, Spinach Balls with Mustard Sauce*

Finger Biscuits, Snow Peas with Lemon-Anchovy Dipping Sauce

Clockwise from top left: Artichoke Hearts with Sauce Rémoulade; White Bean Shrimp Salad; Crespelle with Italian Sausage and Salsa Balsamella; Squid, Fennel and Avocado Salad; Roasted Stuffed Peppers with Anchovies

Pesto Pizza Bread, Stuffed Veal Roll
with Hazelnuts in Aspic

Terrine of Garden Vegetables

Terrine of Venison Campagne

From The Summit at Harrah's of Lake Tahoe.

10 to 12 servings

1 pound venison, cut into ¼-inch dice
½ pound veal, cut into ¼-inch dice
2 tablespoons Cognac

2 tablespoons (¼ stick) butter
2 tablespoons chopped shallot
2 tablespoons chopped onion
1½ bay leaves, crushed
½ teaspoon chopped garlic
Pinch *each* of thyme, marjoram, basil, coriander, mace, cinnamon, ground cloves, black pepper, ground red pepper and white pepper
Freshly grated ginger and nutmeg

¾ pound (12 ounces) fatback (or salt pork simmered 10 minutes to remove excess salt and drained), cut into ¼-inch dice
2 ounces pork or beef liver
2 ounces sweetbreads or brains
6 tablespoons all purpose flour

2 eggs
¼ cup whipping cream
¼ cup Calvados or applejack
2 tablespoons dry Madeira
2 ounces smoked ham, cut into ¼-inch dice
2 ounces pickled tongue, cut into ¼-inch dice
2 ounces pistachio nuts, shelled
2 ounces pimientos, cut into ¼-inch dice
1 ounce truffles, cut into ¼-inch dice (juices reserved)
2 teaspoons salt

1 tablespoon butter

½ pound fatback, sliced ⅛ inch thick

Combine venison, veal and Cognac in large bowl and let stand at room temperature for about 1 hour.

Melt 2 tablespoons butter in medium skillet over medium-high heat. Add shallot, onion, bay leaves, garlic, herbs and spices and sauté until vegetables are translucent. Set aside.

Transfer half of venison mixture to another large bowl. Add 2 ounces fatback or salt pork, pork or beef liver, sweetbreads or brains and shallot mixture and blend lightly. Add to processor in batches and mix until finely ground (or use meat grinder with fine blade). Return mixture to large bowl. Add remaining venison and veal, 10 ounces fatback, flour, eggs, whipping cream, Calvados or applejack, Madeira, ham, tongue, pistachios, pimientos and truffles and mix well. Season with salt to taste.

Melt 1 tablespoon butter in medium saucepan over medium-high heat. Add 2 tablespoons venison mixture and sauté until cooked through. Taste (should be slightly salty); adjust seasoning of uncooked mixture.

Preheat oven to 400°F. Line bottom and sides of 1-quart loaf pan with thin slices of fatback. Spoon venison mixture evenly into mold. Top with layer of fatback. Cover mold with foil. Set in large pan. Add enough boiling water to pan to come ¾ up sides of mold. Bake until juices run clear, about 1½ hours.

Remove mold from water bath and transfer to shallow baking pan. Set another 1-quart loaf pan on top and weight with heavy object (a brick wrapped in aluminum foil works well). Let cool. Refrigerate (with weight) overnight.

Just before serving, dip mold in hot water to within ½ inch of rim for 5 to 10 seconds. Quickly run sharp knife around inside of mold and immediately invert onto platter.

Rabbit Terrine

10 servings

Stock

Bones from 5- to 6-pound rabbit
1 veal knuckle, cracked
3 large onions
2 carrots
1 leek
1 cup dry white wine
1 cup water
½ teaspoon freshly ground pepper
2 or 3 pinches *each* of rosemary and thyme
Bouquet garni (parsley, bay leaf and chervil)
Salt

Forcemeat

1 5- to 6-pound rabbit, boned (about 2 pounds meat)
½ pound veal leg
¼ pound ham, chopped
¼ pound lean belly of pork, chopped
¼ pound pork back fat, chopped
½ cup brandy
2 teaspoons salt
Pinch *each* of rosemary and thyme

1 pound pork fat, cut into sheets ⅛ inch thick (for lining the terrine)

For stock: Combine all ingredients except salt in large pot. Bring to boil, skimming off foam as it rises to surface. Reduce heat and simmer 1 hour. Strain. Return liquid to saucepan and reduce by half over high heat. Add salt to taste.

For forcemeat: While stock is cooking, chop most of the rabbit meat and the veal, reserving some large pieces of both. Combine chopped rabbit and veal with remaining ingredients for forcemeat and marinate until stock is done.

Preheat oven to 325°F. Line 2-quart terrine, pâté mold or loaf pan with pork fat sheets, reserving some for top. Alternate layers of forcemeat with the pieces of rabbit and veal, beginning and ending with forcemeat. Cover with remaining sheets of pork fat. Pour ¼ cup reduced stock over top. Cover with foil, set in roasting pan and pour hot water into pan. Bake until set, about 2 hours. Remove from oven and cool. Weight top and refrigerate overnight, until stock is jellied and fat is firm.

2 🌶 Salads and Cold Platters

The earliest salads, so food historians tell us, were simply fresh greens dipped in salt and eaten without further adornment. Salads have certainly come a long way, as the following collection of appetizers tantalizingly demonstrates. There are salads with all kinds of vegetables, fruits and nuts, cheeses and eggs, seafoods, poultry and meats; salads casually tossed together and formally arranged; salads lightly coated with dressings and steeped in marinades. But all of them, like that ancestral salad, have in common their lightness and freshness of taste and remarkable ease of preparation.

The easiest salad appetizers of all—crudités—do not even really need a recipe. Any selection of fresh young garden produce, left whole when small enough or cut into uniform pieces, makes a spectacular appetizer platter for a sit-down meal or a casual buffet. Whole button mushrooms, cherry tomatoes, snow pea pods, Belgian endive leaves; sticks or slices of zucchini, carrots, celery, juliennes of jícama, beet, celery root: the choice of flavors, textures and colors is as excitingly varied as a painter's palette. And accompaniments for dipping may range from do-it-yourself vinaigrette fixings—olive oil, vinegar, salt and pepper—to any of the dressings on the following pages, to many of the dips, spreads and mousses in the first chapter of this volume.

Most of the recipes for salads and cold platters that follow are what the French would call *salades composées,* meaning simply that they are composed of several different kinds of ingredients. Some are molded, such as the Tomato Aspic with Water Chestnuts on page 29. Others, including the popular Italian beef Carpaccio (page 42) and the Scandinavian Gravlax on page 38, are so substantial that they could double as luncheon entrees. Still others fall into the more familiar category of "arranged" salads, which can be anything from Crab Chantilly with Papaya (page 38) to an exotic Vietnamese salad of meat, seafood and vegetables (page 44).

Two recipes in this chapter, while simple in their ingredients and their lack of actual cooking, will nevertheless require some considerable time and effort. The Artichoke Tree on page 33 and the Fresh Fruit Cascade on page 34 are both elaborate edible constructions of fresh produce. With a little patience, however, they are still easy to make, and the time spent on them will pay off in spectacular centerpieces for an appetizer buffet.

 Vegetables and Fruits

Salad Kensington

25 servings

3 pounds sugar snap peas, Chinese long beans or green beans, cut into 2-inch pieces

2 cups loosely packed watercress, washed, dried and tops cut into 2-inch pieces

½ crenshaw melon, honeydew melon or cantaloupe (about 2 pounds), seeded, sliced into ½ × 2⅛-inch pieces and drained

1 cup Citronnade Dressing (see following recipe)
Juice of 3 limes

½ cup toasted pine nuts or toasted slivered almonds

Blanch peas or beans in boiling salted water over medium-high heat until crisp-tender, 3 to 4 minutes. Drain. Transfer to medium bowl, cover and refrigerate.

To serve, combine watercress, peas and melon in large salad bowl and toss lightly. Add dressing and lime juice and toss gently. Sprinkle with nuts.

Citronnade Dressing

Makes 1 cup

1 egg yolk
1 tablespoon Dijon mustard
1 garlic clove, crushed
1 tablespoon fresh lemon juice
1 tablespoon white wine vinegar

¼ teaspoon salt
⅛ teaspoon freshly ground pepper
¾ cup vegetable oil

Combine all ingredients except oil in medium mixing bowl and blend well. Gradually add oil, whisking constantly until well blended. Cover and refrigerate until ready to serve.

Cauliflower, Carrot and Squash Salad

25 servings

1 large head cauliflower, cut into florets 1 to 1½ inches long
1 bunch carrots, cut diagonally into slices ¼ inch thick
1 pound yellow crookneck squash, trimmed, halved and cut into ½-inch pieces

1 cup Citronnade Dressing (see preceding recipe)

Bring salted water to boil in large saucepan over medium-high heat. Add cauliflower and cook until crisp-tender, about 3 minutes. Remove with slotted spoon and immediately plunge into ice water to stop cooking process. Drain well and set aside. Repeat for carrot, cooking 3 minutes, and squash, cooking until crisp-tender. When cool, combine vegetables in large bowl and toss with dressing. Cover and refrigerate overnight.

Marinated Vegetable Medley

10 to 12 servings

1 15-ounce can flageolets, drained (green kidney beans)
1 10-ounce package frozen baby peas, cooked and drained

1 8-ounce jar baby carrots, drained
1 cup vinaigrette

Combine all ingredients and refrigerate for at least 1 hour. Serve chilled.

Mushrooms Pactole

24 servings

2 cups (1 pint) whipping cream
2 cups mayonnaise (preferably homemade)
4 small garlic cloves, crushed
¼ cup finely chopped fresh parsley
¼ cup white wine vinegar
¼ cup fresh lemon juice
8 teaspoons chopped fresh basil or 2 teaspoons dried, crumbled

4 teaspoons Worcestershire sauce
4 teaspoons Sherry
1 teaspoon salt
¼ teaspoon freshly ground pepper
4 pounds fresh mushrooms, washed, stemmed and thinly sliced (reserve 20 to 24 slices for garnish)
Lettuce leaves (garnish)

Beat cream in large bowl of electric mixer until firm but not stiff. Beat in mayonnaise, garlic, parsley, vinegar, lemon juice, basil, Worcestershire, Sherry, salt and pepper. Gently mix in mushrooms. Line large serving platter with lettuce leaves. Mound mushroom mixture in center and garnish top with reserved mushroom slices.

Beet Salad

6 servings

1 8¼-ounce jar diced pickled beets
1 finely chopped medium onion
½ cup finely chopped pickled herring

2 hard-cooked eggs, diced

1 hard-cooked egg yolk, sieved

Drain beets and reserve juice. Mix beets with onion, herring and hard-cooked eggs. Add 3 tablespoons reserved beet liquid and mix gently.
Garnish with sieved yolk. Serve cold.

Tomato Aspic with Water Chestnuts

This crunchy tomato aspic can be prepared a day or two ahead.

6 to 8 servings

Aspic
6 cups tomato juice
2 cups coarsely chopped onion
1 cup coarsely chopped celery
8 fresh basil leaves or 1 teaspoon dried, crumbled
⅓ cup Worcestershire sauce
1 small chili or ⅛ teaspoon red pepper flakes

Salt
¾ cup dry white wine
3 tablespoons unflavored gelatin

1 cup thinly sliced water chestnuts
½ cup thinly sliced green onion
5 tablespoons fresh lemon juice

🌱 *Aspic for Glazing, Molding and Garnishing*

Aspic—from the Greek word for shield—refers to a versatile method of serving and garnishing cold foods with gelatin. Aspic itself is a simple concoction of unflavored gelatin and liquid, but the term has myriad applications, many of which can be elegant standbys for warm-weather entertaining. A beautifully garnished mousse of vegetables or seafood, aspic-glazed ham or country pâté or a bountiful platter of cold meat lying on a glistening bed of cubed aspic can be prepared ahead and left in the refrigerator.

The techniques for working with gelatin are always the same: Gelatin must first be *softened* in a cold substance, then *dissolved* in a hot substance, and then *chilled*.

Stock-Based Aspic

Aspic made from clarified stock is used for glazing or decorating meat, fish or other savory foods. It also forms the basis for many gelled mousses.

Makes 1 quart

1 quart Clarified Stock (see following recipe)	2 envelopes (2 tablespoons) unflavored gelatin

If starting with cold stock, pour into 3-quart saucepan. Sprinkle gelatin over surface and stir over low heat until liquid is clear and gelatin is dissolved.

If starting with hot stock, sprinkle gelatin over ¼ cup cold water or dry white wine to soften, then add to stock. Stir mixture over low heat until gelatin is dissolved.

At this stage, aspic is ready to be molded and chilled or partially gelled for use as a glaze.

Clarified Stock

Egg white and egg shells draw together particles that cloud the stock.

Makes 1 quart

1½ quarts cold, fat-free homemade stock	2 egg shells, slightly crushed but still intact
2 egg whites, lightly beaten	Cheesecloth

Place stock in 3-quart saucepan. Stir beaten egg whites into stock. Add egg shells. Heat *slowly* to boiling, about 15 to 20 minutes, stirring 2 or 3 times during first few minutes (slow heating allows sediment to rise to the surface of the stock—do not stir again). When stock boils, remove from heat. Let stock stand undisturbed 15 minutes. Line a strainer with about 12 layers of cheesecloth wrung out in cold water. Pour stock through strainer. Allow to stand undisturbed 15 minutes. Cool, uncovered, or use immediately.

Vinaigrette
¼ cup olive oil
3 tablespoons finely chopped onion
2 tablespoons red wine vinegar
2 tablespoons finely chopped fresh basil or 1 teaspoon dried, crumbled

1 tablespoon Dijon mustard
Salt and freshly ground pepper

8 ripe tomatoes, blanched, peeled, cored and sliced (garnish)

For aspic: Combine tomato juice, onion, celery, basil, Worcestershire, chili and salt in large saucepan and bring to boil over medium-high heat. Reduce heat, cover and cook until celery and onion are soft, about 30 minutes. Remove mixture from heat.

Combine wine and gelatin in small bowl and let stand for 10 minutes.

Note: If any other liquid (such as wine or tomato juice) is to be used in aspic, add to stock before clarifying. Proportions of liquid to egg whites (3 cups to 1 white) are approximately the same.

Ways to Use Stock-Based Aspic

Glazing or Coating. Set saucepan filled with hot gelatin mixture in bowl of ice cubes. Stir constantly until gelatin is consistency of unbeaten egg white—approximately 10 to 15 minutes. Put chilled meat, fish or fowl on rack placed on baking sheet. Spoon gelatin mixture over, coating thinly. When aspic is tacky to the touch, arrange decorations (if any) on top. Allow aspic to set. Spoon more gelatin mixture over decorations (if aspic has become too firm, reheat and rechill). Refrigerate until glaze is firm, about 1 hour.

Diced Aspic. Pour warm aspic into flat pan to depth of ¾ inch. Refrigerate until firmly set. Gently turn onto cutting surface. Cut into strips, then dice coarsely. Arrange cubes on platter around cold fowl, meat or fish.

Aspic Cutouts. Cut flat slab of aspic into shapes with cookie or canapé cutters. Use spatula dipped in cold water to transfer to serving platter.

Hints

- While chilling aspic, stir occasionally to prevent sides from gelling faster than the center.
- If aspic sets too quickly, simply reheat in top of double boiler or over low heat to return to liquid stage; then rechill.
- Lightly oiling a mold before adding gelatin facilitates unmolding.
- Quick stock utilizing canned broths (chicken broth or clam juice, for example) can be used to make Clarified Stock. Try this one:

Quick Beef Stock. Combine 3 10½-ounce cans beef broth, ½ cup *each* chopped carrot and onion, ½ cup Port or Madeira, bouquet garni of 4 parsley sprigs, ¼ cup celery leaves, ¼ bay leaf, ¼ teaspoon *each* dried thyme and marjoram. Simmer gently for 20 to 30 minutes, then strain.

Puree tomato mixture in batches in food processor or blender. Strain into large saucepan. Place over low heat. Add gelatin mixture, stirring until gelatin is completely dissolved.

Rinse (but do not dry) 2-quart round mold. Pour in half of aspic. Refrigerate mixture until partially set.

Mix water chestnuts, onion and lemon juice in small bowl and toss lightly. Drain well. Spread water chestnut mixture evenly over top of partially set aspic. Spoon remaining aspic into mold. Refrigerate until firm, at least 3 hours.

For vinaigrette: Combine olive oil, onion, vinegar, basil, mustard, salt and pepper in container with tight-fitting lid and shake to blend well.

Just before serving, dip mold briefly into hot water. Invert onto platter. Surround with tomato slices. Carefully spoon vinaigrette over tomatoes.

Jerusalem Artichoke Salad

25 servings

2½ cups olive oil
1¼ cups white wine vinegar
⅔ cup finely chopped green onion
2 tablespoons salt
1 tablespoon dried tarragon, crumbled

2½ teaspoons freshly ground pepper

5 pounds Jerusalem artichokes, washed, unpeeled, cut into ⅛-inch julienne

Combine oil, vinegar, onion, salt, tarragon and pepper in jar with tight-fitting lid and shake well. Refrigerate until ready to use.

To serve, arrange artichokes on large platter and spoon dressing over.

Avocado Gazpacho Mold

8 to 10 servings

1 28-ounce can plum tomatoes, undrained
1 large cucumber, peeled, seeded and cut into chunks
1 green pepper, seeded and cut into chunks
1 small onion, quartered
2 tablespoons olive oil
2 tablespoons tomato paste
2 teaspoons salt
1 teaspoon Worcestershire sauce
½ teaspoon celery seed

¼ teaspoon ground red pepper

2 envelopes unflavored gelatin
⅓ cup dry white wine

1 large avocado, peeled and pitted
½ large cucumber, peeled, seeded and chopped

Parsley sprigs, lemon slices or wedges and avocado slices (garnish)

Lightly oil 1½-quart ring mold; set aside. Combine first 10 ingredients in processor or blender and mix until pureed. Press through sieve into bowl.

Combine gelatin and wine in small bowl set over hot water and dissolve. Stir into puree and mix well. Pour half into mold (leave remainder at room temperature) and place in freezer until mixture is set, about 20 minutes.

Thinly slice avocado. Arrange over gelled mixture. Sprinkle with chopped cucumber. Carefully pour remaining puree over top. Cover with plastic wrap and refrigerate overnight.

To serve, unmold onto platter and garnish with parsley, lemon and avocado.

Artichoke Hearts with Sauce Rémoulade

12 servings

18 artichokes
1 lemon, halved

Sauce Rémoulade
¼ cup red wine vinegar (preferably aceto balsamico*)
4 egg yolks
8 anchovy fillets
2 tablespoons capers, rinsed and drained
4 cornichons
2 shallots, halved
2 garlic cloves

2 teaspoons Dijon mustard
8 parsley sprigs
1 tablespoon fresh tarragon, minced or 1 teaspoon dried, crumbled
1 tablespoon fresh chervil, minced or 1 teaspoon dried, crumbled
1¼ cups olive oil
3 tablespoons fresh lemon juice
1 teaspoon salt
½ teaspoon freshly ground pepper

1 hard-cooked egg yolk, sieved
(garnish)

For artichokes: Break off stem of artichoke and rub exposed area with lemon. Starting from base, bend each leaf back and snap off where it breaks naturally. Cut off tight cone of leaves above heart. Trim and shape heart carefully with knife until no dark green areas remain. Rub with lemon. Repeat procedure with remaining artichokes.

Steam hearts until tender and easily pierced with knife, about 20 to 30 minutes. Drain well. Let cool on rack. Scoop out chokes with spoon and discard. Cut hearts into quarters. Transfer to bowl, cover and refrigerate until ready to use. *(Can be prepared 1 to 2 days ahead to this point.)*

For sauce: Puree first 11 ingredients in processor or blender. Transfer to bowl. Whisk in oil 1 drop at a time until mixture is thickened and sauce is consistency of mayonnaise. Add lemon juice, salt and pepper and blend well.

Just before serving, add sauce to artichoke hearts and mix well. Turn into serving bowl. Sprinkle with egg yolk.

*Available at specialty food stores.

Artichoke Tree

This attractive presentation can be completely assembled one day ahead, wrapped in damp toweling and stored in a cool area (do not refrigerate). Position the artichokes and lemons with skewers all over the tree before hammering them into place. Each artichoke is secured with three skewers so the leaves can be removed easily. Serve with Lemon Cream (see following recipe) for dipping.

18 to 36 servings

Equipment
   1 polystyrene cone with base 7 inches in diameter trimmed to height of 13 inches
   U-shaped florist pins
   9-inch heavy-duty wood skewers
   Hammer
   Round serving tray at least 12 inches in diameter

Produce
   3 large heads chicory or curly leaf lettuce, tough cores removed
  18 medium artichokes, cooked
  16 to 18 large lemons

To assemble: Cover cone completely with chicory or lettuce, attaching with florist pins. Set cone on serving tray.

Attach 6 artichokes around base of cone by skewering each straight through center and once on each side for a total of 3 skewers; *this is for positioning only, so do not push skewers all the way into cone at this point.* Attach 1 artichoke at very top of cone using 3 more skewers. Fill in sides with remaining artichokes, spacing evenly and leaving room between for lemons.

Attach lemons as desired by skewering each lengthwise straight through center, *but do not push skewers all the way into cone.* Check to see that both artichokes and lemons are positioned exactly where you want them, then carefully hammer skewers into place.

Lemon Cream

A refreshing dip for artichokes. Can be made up to three days ahead.

Makes 4 cups

   2 cups mayonnaise
   2 cups sour cream
   ¼ cup fresh lemon juice
  2½ teaspoons finely grated lemon peel
   2 teaspoons white horseradish

   2 teaspoons Dijon mustard
   1 teaspoon salt

Combine all ingredients in large bowl and blend. Cover and refrigerate. Adjust seasoning before serving.

Fresh Fruit Cascade

18 to 36 servings

Equipment
7 polystyrene rounds (each 12 inches in diameter and 2 inches thick)
9-inch heavy-duty wood skewers
Hammer
Round platter or board at least 24 inches in diameter (will not show when centerpiece is completed)

Fruit
9 pineapples 6 to 7 inches high (plus crown)

1½ watermelons (about 8 inches in diameter)
12 pounds grapes (green and red)
12 pints large strawberries (long-stemmed preferred)
3 cantaloupes, peeled, seeded and cut into 1¼-inch pieces
2 honeydew melons, peeled, seeded and cut into 1¼-inch pieces

For framework: Stack 4 polystyrene rounds on left edge of platter or board. Hammer 3 skewers vertically to secure. Place another round on top and secure with another skewer.

Cut remaining polystyrene rounds in half. Place ½ round on back half of top of stack for a step effect. Stack remaining 3 halves on right edge of platter, at a slight angle to taller stack.

To assemble: Cut bottom ¼ off 1 whole pineapple so it is level. Center on ½ round at top of taller stack and anchor firmly with skewers. Cut 2 of the remaining pineapples in half vertically. Attach upright rounded side out around outside of taller stack, spacing evenly at least 2 inches above base.

Make 3 watermelon baskets by cutting 6-inch lengths from ends of melons in zigzag pattern. Carefully hollow out baskets, cutting fruit into 1¼-inch pieces; set melon aside. Skewer 1 basket to front of taller stack under 1 of the pineapple halves. Center second basket on top of shorter stack and skewer firmly into place. Set last basket on level just below whole pineapple on top of taller stack and skewer securely.

Fill in empty spaces between and around both polystyrene stacks with clusters of grapes, securing with skewers; *do not hammer skewers into place until grapes are exactly where you want them.*

Fill watermelon baskets with strawberries. Set cascade on buffet table where it is to be displayed. Cut remaining pineapples in half lengthwise. Carefully hollow out, cutting fruit into 1¼-inch pieces. Arrange pineapple shells around base of platter or board. Fill with pineapple and melon pieces.

 *Seafood*

Bird's Nest

6 *servings*

1 tablespoon capers, rinsed and drained
1 medium onion, chopped
¼ cup finely chopped herring or anchovy fillets
3 tablespoons chopped fresh parsley

½ cup diced cooked beets
1 egg yolk
  Swedish flatbread

Mound capers in center of serving bowl or round platter. Surround with rings of onion, herring, parsley and beets.

Place egg yolk in shell in egg cup at side of bowl. The custom is for the guest of honor to pour the yolk into the "nest" and mix all ingredients together. Serve with Swedish flatbread.

Squid, Fennel and Avocado Salad

12 *servings*

2 tablespoons olive oil
1½ pounds fresh squid, cleaned, patted dry and cut into thin rings
3 tablespoons fresh lemon juice
1 teaspoon freshly grated lemon peel
½ cup plus 1 tablespoon olive oil
1 large garlic clove, minced
3 tablespoons minced green onion
3 tablespoons minced fresh fennel bulb or minced Belgian endive*
2 teaspoons minced fresh sweet anise or ⅔ teaspoon pulverized fennel seed

¾ teaspoon salt
⅓ teaspoon freshly ground pepper
2 large avocados, peeled, pitted and cubed
3 small fennel bulbs,* cut lengthwise into strips or 3 small heads Belgian endive,* cut lengthwise into strips or 3 small heads romaine lettuce, cut lengthwise into strips
1 lemon, scored and thinly sliced (garnish)

Heat olive oil in heavy skillet over low heat. Add squid and cook until tender, about 5 minutes. Set aside.

Combine lemon juice and peel in bowl. Whisk in olive oil 1 drop at a time until mixture is thickened. Stir in garlic, onion, fennel, anise, salt, pepper and squid and mix well. Cover and refrigerate for 2 days, stirring occasionally.

Add avocado to salad several hours before serving; mix well. Drain off excess dressing, if necessary. Mound salad in center of round serving platter. Arrange strips of fennel, endive or romaine around salad in spoke pattern. Set 1 lemon slice between each spoke and 1 in center of salad. Cover and refrigerate. Let stand at room temperature 1 hour before serving.

*Omit these ingredients if out of season.

White Bean Shrimp Salad

This salad is equally good prepared with prawns, crayfish or crab.

12 servings

1½ pounds shrimp, shelled and deveined (reserve shells)
2 carrots, quartered
2 celery stalks, quartered
1 large onion, quartered
2 garlic cloves
8 parsley sprigs
1 large bay leaf
2 strips lemon peel
2 whole cloves
1 teaspoon coriander seed
¾ teaspoon fresh rosemary or ¼ teaspoon dried, crumbled
1 cup dry white wine or vermouth
8 cups water

4 ounces dried white beans, soaked overnight in cold water and drained

¼ cup fresh lemon juice
2 tablespoons Dijon mustard
⅓ cup olive oil
3 tablespoons minced sweet red onion
1 tablespoon minced fresh parsley (preferably Italian flat leaf)
2 teaspoons salt
1 teaspoon freshly ground pepper

6 tomatoes
Salt

12 black olives (preferably Italian)
Watercress

Combine shrimp shells, carrot, celery, onion, garlic, parsley, bay leaf, lemon peel, cloves, coriander, rosemary, wine and water in 6-quart saucepan and bring to boil over high heat. Reduce heat and simmer until liquid is reduced to 2 cups, about 1 hour. Strain into 3-quart saucepan. Heat until liquid is barely simmering. Add shrimp and cook until just pink, about 4 minutes. Transfer shrimp to large bowl using slotted spoon, reserving cooking liquid.

Combine shrimp cooking liquid with enough cold water to equal 4 times the amount of drained beans. Transfer liquid to Dutch oven or other large saucepan and bring to boil. Add beans, reduce heat and simmer until tender, about 3 hours. Drain well, reserving 2 tablespoons cooking liquid. Add beans to shrimp and toss mixture lightly.

Combine reserved 2 tablespoons liquid, lemon juice and mustard in small bowl. Whisk in olive oil 1 drop at a time until mixture is thickened. Add onion, parsley, salt and pepper and mix well. Add to shrimp and beans and toss lightly. Cover and chill 2 days; stir occasionally.

Using tip of sharp knife, cut zigzag around center of each tomato, then gently pull apart. Squeeze out seeds. Hollow out halves using sharp knife. Coarsely chop pulp and blend into shrimp mixture. Cover salad and refrigerate. Sprinkle tomatoes with salt and invert on rack. Let drain 1 hour. Set aside.

About 1 hour before serving, drain excess dressing from salad. Toss salad lightly and spoon into tomato halves, mounding in center. Top each with olive. Arrange on watercress-lined platter.

Marinated Shrimp and Cucumber

6 servings

1 medium cucumber, peeled and diced
½ pound cooked, chopped small shrimp
6 tablespoons vinegar

¼ teaspoon ground coriander or ½ teaspoon dried dillweed
2 tablespoons vegetable oil
Salt and freshly ground pepper

Combine all ingredients and chill. Serve cold.

Crudité Salad with Scallops and Shrimp

A light main course that doubles as a nonwiltable salad. All vegetables may be chopped a day ahead. Cook seafood up to 24 hours ahead and marinate.

12 servings

1½ pounds uncooked medium shrimp
1½ pounds sea scallops, halved and trimmed of small connective tissue

  2 cups light olive oil
⅔ cup white wine vinegar
  4 green onions, minced
  2 garlic cloves, minced
    Salt and freshly ground pepper
  1 head cauliflower, broken into small florets

½ head red cabbage, shredded
  3 large carrots, shredded
  2 medium zucchini, shredded
  1 10-ounce package frozen baby peas, thawed
  4 celery stalks, peeled and chopped
½ medium red onion, minced

  1 tablespoon Dijon mustard
  1 head chicory, rinsed and dried

Place shrimp in saucepan, cover with cold water and bring to simmer over medium heat. As soon as shrimp turn pink, remove with slotted spoon. Let cool briefly, then shell. Place scallops in saucepan, cover with cold water and cook just below simmer until almost firm, about 2 minutes. Remove with slotted spoon. *(The most important factor here is not to overcook the shellfish. Scallops should still be slightly soft and shrimp just barely firm.)*

Combine oil, vinegar, green onion and garlic with salt and pepper to taste. Place seafood in bowl and pour half the dressing over. Cover and refrigerate shrimp-scallop mixture and remaining dressing. Combine next 7 vegetables, cover and refrigerate.

Shortly before serving, add mustard to remaining dressing and pour into serving bowl. Arrange chicory leaves on large platter. Pile vegetables in a ring around outer edge. Drain seafood and mound in center of ring. Cover with plastic wrap and refrigerate until ready to serve.

Shrimp in Green Cheese Sauce

6 servings

1 pound cooked medium shrimp, shelled and chilled
1 small ripe avocado, peeled and mashed
1 3-ounce package cream cheese, softened
1 teaspoon lime juice

Dash of tequila
Salt and freshly ground pepper

1 tablespoon minced fresh cilantro or parsley (garnish)

Arrange shrimp on serving platter. Combine avocado, cream cheese, lime juice, tequila, salt and pepper and blend thoroughly.

Serve sauce over shrimp or on the side, garnished with cilantro or parsley.

Quick Glassblower's Herring

6 servings

1 12-ounce jar marinated herring
1 medium carrot, cooked and sliced
1 large red onion, thinly sliced

1 teaspoon mustard seed
½ teaspoon peppercorns

Pour marinated herring with liquid into bowl. Add carrot, onion, mustard seed and peppercorns. Refrigerate overnight, turning several times. Serve chilled. Remove peppercorns, if desired.

Crab Chantilly with Papaya

2 servings

¼ cup mayonnaise
1 tablespoon minced pimientos
1 tablespoon minced fresh parsley
1 teaspoon fresh lemon juice
  Salt and freshly ground pepper
½ cup whipping cream, whipped

2 cups cooked crabmeat
  Lettuce leaves
1 papaya, peeled, quartered, seeded
  and thinly sliced or 4 fresh
  pineapple spears
  Fresh mint sprigs (garnish)

Combine mayonnaise, pimientos, parsley, lemon juice, salt and pepper in small bowl. Fold in whipped cream. Add crabmeat. Arrange lettuce leaves on plate. Mound crabmeat mixture in center. Surround with papaya slices. Garnish with mint. Serve immediately.

Ceviche

6 servings

1 pound fillet of sole or similar fish,
  cut into bite-size pieces
¼ cup lime juice

1 large tomato, peeled, seeded and
  diced
1 large red onion, coarsely chopped
2 2-ounce cans chopped jalapeño
  peppers

¼ cup olive oil
¼ cup minced fresh parsley or
  cilantro
  Salt and freshly ground pepper

Sprinkle fish with lime juice and marinate in refrigerator for 8 to 12 hours or overnight, turning occasionally. Drain and reserve juice.

Combine fish with all remaining ingredients and sprinkle with reserved juice. Serve chilled.

Gravlax

40 to 80 servings

1 8- to 10-pound salmon, cut
  horizontally and boned but not
  skinned
1 cup sugar
1⅓ cups coarse salt
  Water

  Crushed white peppercorns
  Fresh dillweed, stems discarded,
  heads cut into 1-inch pieces

  Thinly sliced black or brown
  bread

Place fish on baking sheet or large shallow platter. Combine sugar and salt with water to make paste. Pat mixture evenly over skin. Sprinkle with pepper and dillweed. Wrap tightly and refrigerate 4 to 6 days, turning fish over on second day.

Transfer to serving platter, slice paper thin and serve with bread.

 *Poultry*

Chicken and Grape Salad

4 servings

2 cooked whole chicken breasts, boned, skinned and diced
4 celery stalks, diced
½ cup slivered almonds, toasted
½ cup sliced seedless green grapes
1 teaspoon fresh lemon juice
  Mayonnaise
  Salt and freshly ground pepper
  Romaine lettuce leaves

1 bunch spinach leaves
2 carrots, thinly sliced
1 cucumber, peeled and sliced
1 cup alfalfa sprouts
4 green onions, diced
  Chilled cooked asparagus (garnish)
  Herb Dressing (see following recipe), optional

Combine chicken, celery, almonds, grapes and lemon juice in small bowl. Add enough mayonnaise to moisten and mix well. Season with salt and pepper. Cover and refrigerate until ready to use. Line 4 individual plates with lettuce and spinach leaves. Arrange carrot, cucumber, alfalfa sprouts and onion around edges. Mound chicken mixture in center. Top with asparagus. Pass dressing separately if desired.

Herb Dressing

Makes about 2 cups

1⅓ cups oil
¼ cup plus 2 tablespoons white wine vinegar
2 tablespoons minced fresh chives
2 tablespoons minced fresh parsley
2 garlic cloves, minced
1 teaspoon dried basil, crumbled
1 teaspoon salt

½ teaspoon dry mustard
½ teaspoon dried oregano, crumbled
½ teaspoon dried tarragon, crumbled
¼ teaspoon freshly ground pepper
  Ground red pepper

Combine all ingredients in jar with tight-fitting lid and shake well. Refrigerate until ready to use.

Turkey Salad with Almonds and Ginger

8 to 10 servings

2½ cups water
2 teaspoons salt
1 cup long-grain brown rice
¼ cup wild rice

½ cup peanut oil
¼ cup tarragon vinegar
2 tablespoons Dijon mustard
1 tablespoon freshly grated ginger

1 teaspoon freshly ground pepper
1 pound cooked turkey, cut into strips or cubes
2 cups cooked peas
½ cup chopped green onion
½ cup sliced almonds, toasted
¼ cup coarsely chopped red bell pepper

Bring water to boil in medium saucepan over high heat. Add salt and rice. Return to boil, reduce heat, cover and simmer until water is absorbed, about 45 minutes.

Whisk oil, vinegar, mustard, ginger and pepper in large bowl. Stir in rice, turkey, peas, onion, almonds and red bell pepper. Serve salad warm or at room temperature.

Chicken Circassian with Walnut Sauce

25 servings

6 whole chicken breasts

6 to 8 cups chicken broth
(preferably homemade)
Bouquet garni (2 carrots, 2
onions, 4 parsley sprigs)

Walnut Sauce
1½ cups shelled walnuts, toasted

½ cup finely chopped onion
3 slices white bread
½ teaspoon paprika
1 teaspoon salt
Pinch of freshly ground pepper

Walnut halves
Parsley sprigs (garnish)

Place chicken breast skin side down on work surface. Using sharp knife, cut through cartilage at wishbone end. Snap back to expose keel bone and remove bone. Cut chicken breast in half through wishbone. Set half aside. Slide blade of small sharp knife under breastbone of other half, loosening meat from bone. Remove all bone and discard. Gently remove fillet (small tender piece easily pulled away from rest of meat). Trim off all skin and excess fat. Cut rest of breast in half lengthwise for 2 more fillets. Repeat procedure for remaining breast half. Repeat for all breasts (you will have 36 pieces).

Combine chicken with bouquet garni and enough broth to cover in large saucepan over medium heat. Reduce heat and simmer until breasts are tender, about 10 minutes. Remove from heat and let chicken cool in stock. Transfer chicken to serving platter using slotted spoon and set aside.

Skim fat from stock and discard. Cook stock over medium heat until thickened and reduced to 1½ cups.

For sauce: Combine walnuts, onion and reduced stock in processor or blender and mix well. Add bread, paprika, salt and pepper and puree until smooth. Transfer puree to bowl.

To serve, spoon puree over chicken pieces, top with walnut halves and garnish with parsley sprigs.

Galantine de Canard à l'Orange

This presentation is directed toward over-achievers. If you are faint-hearted, short of time, interested in budget dishes or plan to serve only a small group, pass this recipe up for now. Should you decide to make it, you will find it spectacular!

25 servings

Marinade
2 cups Harvey's Bristol Cream
Sherry
1½ cups Cointreau
5 tablespoons salt
3 large garlic cloves, finely minced
Finely minced peel of 4 oranges

2 5-pound ducklings

18 ounces fresh pork back fat
14 ounces lean veal (flank preferred)
14 ounces lean pork (shoulder butt
preferred)

18 ounces boiled or Virginia ham
9 ounces boiled tongue

Poaching Stock
4 quarts rich homemade chicken
stock or 6 quarts canned stock
3 oranges, quartered
2 bay leaves
Reserved duck carcasses and
trimmings

2 eggs, lightly beaten

4 truffles (optional)

Glaze
3 tablespoons honey
3 tablespoons light soy sauce
3 tablespoons dry white wine

For marinade: Blend all ingredients in large mixing bowl.

Carefully bone 1 duckling. Begin by splitting along backbone, then with a very sharp knife separate skin and meat from carcass, cutting at all times against the carcass. Extreme care should be taken, particularly when separating skin from breast cartilage, not to cut the skin. Cut off wing tips, but otherwise leave wings intact. Bone out legs. Reserve the carcass and trimmings, to be used for preparation of stock.

Place duck skin side down. Remove excess fat and skin in neck area. Cut all meat from skin. Turn leg pockets inside out. Put skin in large shallow baking dish.

Remove breasts and legs from remaining duck. Wrap skin in plastic and refrigerate. Cut breast meat from both ducks lengthwise into julienne strips about ³⁄₈ inch thick. (The total weight should be about 22 ounces.) Add to baking dish; pour half of marinade over.

Coarsely chop leg meat either by hand or in processor. (The total weight will approximate 11 ounces.) Coarsely chop pork fat by hand. Coarsely chop veal and lean pork in processor. By hand, mix duck leg meat, pork fat, pork and veal and place in bowl with remaining marinade. Cover and chill overnight.

Cut ham and tongue into long julienne strips between ¼ and ³⁄₈ inch thick. Add to baking dish with duck skin. Cover and refrigerate overnight.

For stock: Combine chicken stock, oranges, bay leaves and reserved duck carcasses and trimmings in stockpot and simmer uncovered 1½ hours. Cool, then cover and refrigerate overnight.

To assemble: Discard layer of solidified fat from stock. Set stock aside.

Fry heaping tablespoon of the ground meats in small skillet. Taste and adjust seasoning as necessary. Add eggs to meat mixture (farce) and blend well.

Spread duck skin side down, making certain that leg pockets are pushed in from the outside (facing you). Take ⅓ of farce and cover skin uniformly. Cover farce lengthwise with julienne of duck. Cover with ⅓ of remaining farce, building up edges at 45° angle. When all layers are in place, a cross section of the duck will appear pyramidal.

Cover farce with julienne of ham. Use a little more than half of the remaining farce to cover. Arrange tongue strips over this layer. Cover with remaining farce. If truffles are being used, arrange on top of pyramid.

Unless one is blessed with 3 hands, the next step may be impossible. Call a friend to help.

Lift duck skin from each side and bring together to close. Using heavy thread, sew skin together until it resembles a whole bird, minus the legs, of course. Truss wings into proper position.

Roll bird tightly in clean towel, which will act as a baster. Cover and poach in *barely* simmering stock 15 minutes per pound, roughly 2 hours. (A fish poacher is ideal for this.) Let cool completely in stock. Unwrap carefully, removing any extraneous fat.

Dry bird carefully and let stand 2 hours. Repair any holes that might have developed during poaching by using pieces of skin from the second duck.

To glaze: Preheat oven to 375°F. Oil a *nonstick* baking sheet. Combine all ingredients for glaze and brush duck generously. Place bird on baking sheet and bake until lightly browned, about 15 minutes, basting with glaze as necessary to promote browning. This is for aesthetics only; watch carefully to avoid over-browning. Remove from oven and chill at least 6 hours before slicing.

Chang's Anise-Smoked Duck

4 to 6 servings

Marinade
  1 small onion
  1 garlic clove
  3 or 4 pieces candied ginger
  3 star anise
  2 tablespoons sugar
  2 tablespoons dark soy sauce
  1 tablespoon brandy
  1 teaspoon salt

  ½ teaspoon freshly ground white
      pepper
  3 quarts water

  1 4½- to 5-pound duck

Smoking Mixture
  2 cups hickory chips, well soaked
  6 star anise
  3 tablespoons sugar

Combine ingredients for marinade except water in blender and mix to pulverize. Pour into 8-quart pot. Add water (use blender to measure so no seasoning is lost). Simmer 15 minutes.

Add duck, tail-first (so cavity fills with liquid). Weight duck with inverted glass pie plate and let simmer 45 minutes. Remove duck. Discard liquid; wipe duck to remove bits of seasoning.

Wash and dry pot. Line with foil and add hickory chips, star anise and sugar. Set duck on rack and smoke over high heat 20 minutes. Turn off heat and let duck cool and smoke settle at least 1 hour. Carve meat into thin slivers.

 *Meats*

Carpaccio (Italian Beef Appetizer)

6 servings

  2 pounds *uncooked* prime beef top
      round, trimmed and thinly sliced
      into 12 to 18 pieces
      Fresh lemon juice
      Olive oil
  2 to 3 tablespoons capers, rinsed,
      drained and minced

  2 to 3 tablespoons minced fresh
      parsley (preferably Italian)
  3 to 4 mushrooms, thinly sliced
      Freshly ground pepper

Gently pound meat on work surface until paper thin. Arrange 2 to 3 slices in center of each serving plate. Sprinkle generously with lemon juice. Brush oil lightly over meat. Combine capers and parsley in small bowl. Top each slice of meat with 1 teaspoon of mixture. Surround meat with 3 to 4 mushroom slices. Season with pepper and serve.

Stuffed Veal Roll with Hazelnuts in Aspic

12 servings

Stuffing
- 1 tablespoon olive oil
- 1 tablespoon butter
- 1 small onion, minced
- 3 ounces ground veal
- 3 ounces ground pork

- ¼ cup whipping cream
- ¼ cup fresh breadcrumbs
- 1 egg, lightly beaten
- 1 ounce freshly grated imported Parmesan cheese
- 1 garlic clove, minced
- 1 tablespoon minced parsley (preferably Italian flat leaf)
- 1 tablespoon fresh thyme, minced or 1 teaspoon dried, crumbled
- 1 teaspoon dried marjoram, crumbled
- ½ teaspoon salt
- ¼ teaspoon freshly ground pepper
- ⅛ teaspoon freshly grated nutmeg

Veal
- 1 5½- to 6-pound veal breast, boned
  Salt and freshly ground pepper
- 2 slices mortadella, halved
- 3 ounces fresh peas, shelled (about 1 cup)

- 1 ounce hazelnuts (about ⅓ cup), roasted and skinned
- 4 hard-cooked eggs, sliced

- 4 tablespoons olive oil
- 4 tablespoons (½ stick) butter
- 1 large onion, thinly sliced
- 1 large carrot, thinly sliced
- 1 celery stalk, thinly sliced

- 1 bouquet garni (10 celery leaves, 1 bay leaf, 2 fresh thyme sprigs or 1 teaspoon dried, 10 parsley sprigs)
- 2 cups veal or chicken stock
- 1 cup Marsala

- 2 cups (or more) veal or chicken stock

- 3 egg whites and shells

- 2 envelopes unflavored gelatin softened in ¼ cup water

- ⅓ cup Marsala

  Chicory or other crisp leafy greens (garnish)
- 12 tomato roses (garnish)

For stuffing: Heat oil and butter in heavy skillet over low heat. Add onion, cover and cook until translucent, about 10 minutes. Add ground veal and pork, increase heat and cook just until browned. Transfer to bowl and let cool.

Add cream, breadcrumbs, egg, Parmesan, garlic, parsley, thyme, marjoram, salt, pepper and nutmeg to stuffing and mix thoroughly.

For veal: Place veal breast boned side up on work surface. Dip mallet in cold water and pound meat until it is of uniform thickness. Sprinkle lightly with salt and pepper. Arrange slices of mortadella over veal, overlapping slightly and leaving 1-inch border on all sides. Cover with stuffing. Sprinkle with peas and hazelnuts. Arrange eggs down center of stuffing and sprinkle with salt and pepper. Roll veal up lengthwise. Carefully sew ends and seam with string, then tie roll securely at 3 intervals to preserve shape.

Combine 2 tablespoons oil and 2 tablespoons butter in roasting pan. Place over low heat. Add onion, carrot and celery, cover and cook until onion is translucent, about 15 minutes. Transfer to plate using slotted spoon.

Preheat oven to 350°F. Heat remaining oil and butter in same pan over medium-high heat. When foam subsides, add meat and brown on all sides. Return vegetables to pan. Add bouquet garni, stock and Marsala and bring to simmer. Cover meat with piece of buttered parchment paper. Cover pan, transfer to oven and roast 45 minutes, basting occasionally. Turn meat over and continue roasting, basting occasionally until veal is tender and juices run yellow when pricked with fork, about 45 minutes to 1¼ hours. Let cool in liquid. Refrigerate overnight.

Remove meat from pan; discard strings. Cut into 12 equal slices. Arrange slices in single layer on rack set over baking sheet or tray. Sprinkle with salt and pepper and refrigerate.

Discard fat from pan. Place pan over medium heat to liquefy juices, then strain liquid into 2-quart saucepan. Add 2 cups veal stock and boil until liquid is reduced to 4 cups. (If flavor is not concentrated enough, add more veal stock and reduce again.)

Beat egg whites and shells in 3- to 4-quart saucepan until foamy. Slowly stir in stock. Place over medium-low heat and slowly bring to gentle simmer, stirring occasionally. When liquid begins to simmer, adjust heat so stock will shudder but not bubble. Stop stirring and let stock stand until egg whites form firm foamy covering over liquid, about 15 minutes. Gently part foam; if liquid is clear, clarifying is complete.

Line fine sieve with 3 layers of dampened cheesecloth or linen kitchen towel. Place softened gelatin in bowl and put sieve over bowl. Gently ladle clarified stock into sieve. *Do not force or shake stock through cloth, just let it drizzle; forcing or stirring could allow some of egg white to pass through cloth and cause stock to become cloudy.*

When all stock has been ladled through cloth, stir with clean spoon to combine with gelatin. Return mixture to saucepan and cook over low heat, stirring constantly until gelatin is completely dissolved. Add Marsala and season to taste with salt and pepper.

Stir gelatin mixture over ice water until aspic is cool and slightly thickened. Paint meat slices with layer of aspic and refrigerate until set, about 20 minutes. Repeat 3 or 4 more times until meat is well covered, stirring aspic over heat if it becomes too thick. Pour remaining aspic into shallow pan and refrigerate until firm. Cut into cubes.

Arrange chicory on serving platter. Place veal over top and surround with aspic cubes. Garnish each slice with tomato rose and refrigerate. Bring to room temperature before serving.

Goi and Banh Phong Tom (Hors d'Oeuvre Salad)

8 to 10 servings

Salad (Goi)
2 tablespoons oil
2 shallots, minced
½ pound pork, cut into very thin ½ × 1-inch slices
¼ pound uncooked shrimp, peeled, deveined and cut in half lengthwise
2 teaspoons fish sauce (nuoc mam)*
Freshly ground pepper

1 3-inch square dried jellyfish*

1½ cups bean sprouts
¼ cup toasted sesame seed
¼ cup toasted peanuts, chopped
3 tablespoons fresh mint leaves, chopped
3 tablespoons fresh coriander leaves, chopped
2 tablespoons Nuoc Cham (see recipe, page 95)
1 carrot, shredded
Shrimp Chips (banh phong tom) (see following recipe)

For salad: Heat oil in large skillet over medium-high heat. Add shallot and sauté until softened. Add pork and stir-fry 2 minutes. Add shrimp, fish sauce and pepper and continue cooking, stirring constantly, until shrimp are opaque. Transfer to large bowl; let cool.

Meanwhile, place jellyfish in small bowl. Cover with hot water and let stand 30 minutes to soften. Drain well; rinse several times under cold water and drain again. Cut into thin strips. Add to shrimp mixture and toss lightly.

Blanch bean sprouts several seconds in boiling water. Drain thoroughly. Add shrimp mixture and toss well. Add all remaining ingredients except Shrimp Chips and toss thoroughly. Arrange Shrimp Chips on platter and top with salad. Serve at room temperature.

Toast sesame seed and peanuts by stirring in small skillet over medium to medium-high heat for about 2 to 3 minutes.

*Can be purchased at oriental markets.

Shrimp Chips

Shrimp Chips are usually served alone as an hors d'oeuvre or as a cracker to accompany salads. They can be purchased ready-made in oriental markets.

Oil	Shrimp Chips

Pour oil into small saucepan to depth of about 1 inch. Place over medium-high heat until very hot. Reduce heat to medium, add chips in batches of 3 and fry, pressing gently with spoon or chopsticks to expand them into larger pieces. Remove with slotted spoon and drain on paper towels. Serve immediately, or store at room temperature in airtight plastic bag up to 1 week.

Slivered Country Ham with Finger Biscuits

Accompany with crocks of coarse mustard (France's Moutarde de Meaux would be ideal), a smooth herbed mustard, pickled watermelon rind and Jerusalem artichoke or green tomato relish to cut the rich saltiness of the ham.

12 servings (plus leftover ham)

Finger Biscuits
- 2 cups all purpose unbleached flour
- 2 cups cake flour (do not use self-rising)
- 1 teaspoon salt
- 2 tablespoons plus 2 teaspoons baking powder
- 8 tablespoons (1 stick) well-chilled unsalted butter

1¼ to 1½ cups chilled milk

1 11- to 14-pound cooked country ham (prepare according to your favorite recipe)
Parsley sprigs

For biscuits: Preheat oven to 425°F. Grease baking sheet. Combine dry ingredients in deep bowl. Using pastry blender, cut in butter until mixture resembles coarse meal. With fork, add milk and toss gently; *do not overmix* (use only enough milk to make dough moist but not wet). Turn onto floured board and gently knead only 2 or 3 times. Roll or pat into rectangle ½ inch thick. Cut into 1-inch squares. Transfer to prepared sheet, spacing about ⅛ inch apart. Bake until puffed and golden, 10 to 15 minutes.

To carve ham: Start at shank end by cutting away a small wedge-shaped piece. Set aside. Now, shave small, paper-thin slices, working toward large end of ham. Place partially carved ham on serving platter and surround with warm ham-filled Finger Biscuits. Accompany with relishes and crocks of mustards. Carve more ham as needed. If desired, garnish platter with fresh parsley.

Depending on size of oven, you may have to prepare two batches of biscuits.

Biscuit dough can be prepared 1 day ahead, wrapped and refrigerated overnight. If baking biscuits ahead, let cool, then slit each on 3 sides. Immediately transfer to airtight plastic bags and freeze (they dry out quickly). Defrost in refrigerator the day before serving. Shortly before serving, warm in 350°F oven about 8 minutes or until biscuits are heated through.

 Grains

Tabbouleh

4 to 6 servings

1 cup bulgur
1 cup boiling water

1 cup finely chopped fresh parsley
½ cup finely grated carrot
½ cup raisins or currants
⅓ cup fresh lemon juice

¼ cup finely chopped fresh mint
¼ cup safflower oil
1 garlic clove, finely minced
½ teaspoon salt
Ground red pepper
Bibb lettuce leaves

Combine bulgur and water in medium bowl and let stand until water is absorbed, about 30 minutes. Set aside.

Meanwhile, combine all remaining ingredients except lettuce in large bowl and mix well. Arrange lettuce leaves on platter. Add bulgur to carrot mixture and toss well. Mound in center of platter and serve.

Cold Mexican Rice

6 servings

2 cups cold cooked rice
1 medium onion, chopped
2 jalapeño peppers, chopped

1 teaspoon whole coriander seed
Salt
¼ cup vinaigrette

Combine ingredients and toss gently. Chill thoroughly before serving.

3 ❧ Cold Hors d'Oeuvres

Almost every country that has a recognizable cuisine has its favorite cold appetizers. In some parts of the world, these morsels are a mainstay of the national diet—the sushi of Japan (page 50) or the stuffed grape leaves of Greece (page 50) come immediately to mind. Elsewhere, such appetizers simply fulfill the literal meaning of the term *hors d'oeuvre*—something "outside the main work," a wonderful addition to the major elements of a meal, a snack.

Many of the recipes in this chapter are composed of savory fillings rolled or stuffed into leaves, mushroom caps or hollowed-out vegetables: "finger food" at its most elegant. There is no end to the imaginative combinations: a creamy mixture of cheeses and seasonings is used to fill the fresh peapods in the recipe on page 48; chopped herring fills hollowed-out cooked beets for a Scandinavian-style appetizer (page 56); and mushrooms are compatible with fillings as diverse as ham (page 57), snails (page 49) and ratatouille (page 49)—or they can become a filling themselves, as in Cucumbers with Mushroom Stuffing (page 48).

Eggs and cheese are ideal ingredients for cold appetizers. The rich, mild flavor and smooth texture of hard-cooked egg yolks makes a superb foil to the many ingredients blended together with them for stuffed eggs (page 54). Cheeses, particularly soft and creamy varieties, are handily molded into cheese balls (page 56) or stuffed into vegetables or fruits: Grapes Stuffed with Bleu Cheese (page 55) is an especially pleasing and refreshing combination.

Some cold snacks are even simpler. Marinated and pickled vegetables (pages 52–53) enliven any appetite with their crisp textures and zesty flavors. And no appetizer buffet would seem complete without nuts, perhaps the most common of simple snacks. But you and your guests are sure to find the nut recipes on pages 57–58 uncommonly delightful.

🍃 *Stuffed Vegetables*

Stuffed Snow Peas

100 appetizers

100 snow peas

Filling
- 1 pound cream cheese, softened
- ¼ cup grated sapsago cheese or freshly grated Parmesan cheese
- 3 tablespoons catsup
- 2 teaspoons dried dillweed
- 1 teaspoon dry mustard
- 1 teaspoon Worcestershire sauce
- ½ to 1 teaspoon salt
- ½ teaspoon freshly ground white pepper

Arrange snow peas in large bowl and cover with boiling water. Let stand about 1 minute. Drain peas well and immediately plunge into ice water. Drain again. Trim ¼ inch from stem end of each pod and discard. Set peas aside.

For filling: Combine all ingredients in large mixing bowl and blend well. Using pastry tube fitted with ¼- to ⅛-inch tip, pipe filling into cut end of each pea pod. Chill until ready to serve.

Jalapeños en Escabeche Stuffed with Peanut Butter

Jalapeños en escabeche (pickled jalapeño peppers), preferably from Mexico

Creamy peanut butter

Cut peppers almost in half lengthwise from tip to stem and remove seeds.* Using pastry tube or spoon, fill each chili with about 1 teaspoon peanut butter. Press halves of each chili together gently and arrange on serving platter.

*It is advisable to wear rubber gloves while handling chilies.

Cucumbers with Mushroom Stuffing

12 appetizers

- 2 thin cucumbers about 7 inches long (ends removed), peeled and cut into slices ¾ inch thick

Stuffing
- ½ pound firm mushrooms, finely chopped
- 1 tablespoon vegetable oil (preferably cold-pressed safflower)
- 1 teaspoon fresh lemon juice
- 1 tablespoon chopped fresh dillweed or 1½ teaspoons dried
  Herb or vegetable salt
  Freshly ground pepper

Lettuce leaves (garnish)

Scoop out centers of each cucumber slice using melon baller; reserve centers. Pat cucumber slices and centers dry with paper towels.

For stuffing: Combine mushrooms, oil and lemon juice in small skillet and cook over high heat 1 minute. Add dillweed, salt and pepper and continue cooking over high heat until liquid evaporates, about 1 to 2 minutes. Transfer mixture to small bowl, cover and refrigerate.

Just before serving, fill cucumber slices with mushroom mixture. Cover with reserved centers. Arrange lettuce on platter and top with stuffed cucumbers.

Stuffing can be prepared 2 to 3 hours ahead.

Snail-Stuffed Mushrooms

6 servings

¼ cup white vinegar
1 garlic clove, minced
¾ cup olive oil
1 teaspoon minced fresh parsley
2 tablespoons coarsely chopped chives

1 7-ounce can (24) snails, drained
24 medium mushroom caps, lightly sautéed in butter or margarine

Combine vinegar, garlic, oil, parsley and 1 tablespoon chives in medium bowl and mix well. Add snails to marinade. Chill for at least 1 hour.

Drain well. Arrange snails in mushroom caps. Sprinkle with remaining chives. Serve cold.

Ratatouille in Raw Mushroom Caps

50 appetizers

1 unpeeled medium eggplant (1¼ pounds), coarsely chopped (7 cups)
3 unpeeled zucchini (1 pound total), coarsely chopped (3 cups)
1 tablespoon salt
6 tablespoons oil (combination olive and peanut or safflower oils)
1 teaspoon dried thyme
½ teaspoon ground coriander
Pinch of cumin

2 medium onions (10 ounces total), finely minced (2 cups)

3 small tomatoes (9 ounces total), peeled, seeded, and chopped (¾ cup)
2 small green or red bell peppers (6 ounces total), seeded and chopped (¾ cup)
2 garlic cloves, minced
Pinch of sugar
⅓ cup minced parsley leaves
½ teaspoon dried basil
Salt and freshly ground pepper
50 large firm white mushrooms, stems removed

Preheat oven to 350°F. Grease 1½-quart heatproof baking dish. Place eggplant and zucchini in large colander and sprinkle with salt. Let stand 30 minutes to drain. Rinse and pat dry with paper towels. Heat 3 tablespoons oil in large skillet over high heat. Add eggplant and zucchini and sauté 1 minute. Cover and continue cooking 3 minutes, shaking pan several times, until vegetables are steamed through. Add thyme, coriander and cumin and blend. Remove from skillet and set aside.

Heat remaining oil in same skillet. Add onion and sauté until soft. Add tomatoes, bell pepper, garlic and sugar. Cover and cook 5 minutes, shaking pan frequently. Remove lid and continue cooking until all liquid is evaporated. Return eggplant and zucchini to skillet with 2 tablespoons parsley, basil, salt and pepper. Transfer to baking dish. Cover and bake 40 minutes. Pour off any excess liquid, or cook quickly, uncovered, over high direct heat until liquid evaporates. Taste and adjust seasoning. Fill each mushroom cap with about 1½ tablespoons ratatouille. Sprinkle with reserved parsley. Serve warm or at room temperature.

Can be prepared several days in advance.

Dolmathes (Stuffed Grape Leaves)

48 to 60 appetizers

¼ cup olive oil
1 medium onion, finely chopped
1 pound lean ground lamb
½ cup short-grain rice
½ cup chopped fresh dillweed or 1 tablespoon dried
⅓ cup pine nuts
¼ cup water
2 tablespoons tomato paste
Freshly ground pepper
Salt (if fresh leaves are used)

1 1-quart jar grape leaves in brine, well rinsed, or about 48 fresh grape leaves, blanched in boiling water 2 to 3 minutes until pliable

¾ cup rich chicken broth
3 tablespoons fresh lemon juice
1 lemon, thinly sliced (garnish)

Heat oil in large skillet. Add onion and sauté until translucent. Add meat, stirring to break into pieces. Add rice, dillweed, pine nuts, water and tomato paste. Season to taste with pepper, and salt, if necessary. Cook over medium heat until water is absorbed, about 10 minutes.

Cover bottom of Dutch oven with layer of grape leaves. Stuff remaining leaves by placing leaf shiny side down on palm of hand with base of leaf toward wrist and tip toward middle finger. Put a spoonful of meat mixture in center. Fold base over stuffing, then fold sides of leaf over (like an envelope), tucking edges in snugly. Roll up and tuck tip of leaf beneath to prevent unrolling. Arrange tip side down in pan.

Add broth to within 1 inch of top layer. Use any leftover leaves to cover top layer. Place plate upside down over top layer and press. Cover and cook over medium heat until rice is tender, about 30 minutes. Sprinkle with lemon juice and cook 5 minutes longer. Let cool to room temperature, or chill thoroughly. Serve garnished with lemon slices.

Stuffed Grape Leaves can be prepared 2 to 3 days before serving and refrigerated, or they may be frozen. If frozen, thaw overnight in refrigerator, then add a little broth or water before gently reheating.

Maki Mono (Rolled Sushi with Gourd or Cucumber)

Purchase a slatted mat (sudaré) to aid in the rolling of the sushi.

48 appetizers

45 to 50 inches kanpyō (dried gourd ribbon)*

½ cup (or more) Dashi (see following recipe)
2 tablespoons soy sauce
2 tablespoons sugar
1½ teaspoons mirin (syrupy rice wine)

3½ tablespoons sushi su (seasoned vinegar)*
2 cups freshly cooked rice (still warm)

4 sheets asakusa nori (dried laver or seaweed)*

1½ teaspoons white sesame seed

½ teaspoon wasabi paste** (green horseradish)
1 thin hothouse cucumber, peeled, halved, seeded and cut julienne

Soy sauce

Combine dried gourd in bowl with enough warm water to cover and let soak about 20 minutes. Squeeze gourd between hands using back and forth motion. Rinse in cold water. Drain well and pat dry.

Combine ½ cup Dashi, soy sauce, sugar, mirin and gourd in medium saucepan over low heat. Cook 15 minutes, adding more Dashi if necessary. Remove from heat; let gourd cool in cooking liquid. Cut into 6-inch lengths and set aside.

Sprinkle vinegar over warm rice and toss, fanning rice with piece of stiff cardboard to avoid condensation. Dampen hands in acidulated water (to prevent rice from sticking). Divide rice mixture evenly and shape into 8 balls. Cover with damp cloth and set aside.

Preheat oven to 250°F. Arrange 4 sheets of nori on baking sheet. Let dry in oven 3 to 4 minutes (or move back and forth over medium-low heat one at a time for about 20 seconds). Cut each dried sheet in half.

Open slatted mat (sudaré) on work surface. Place piece of laver on top. Dampen hands and spread 1 rice ball over laver. Arrange 2 gourd strips over rice. Flip edge of mat over filling and press down lightly. Roll up sushi, using mat as aid. Remove sushi from mat and set seam side down. Repeat 3 times for a total of 4 gourd sushi.

Toast sesame seed about 1 minute in heavy (thoroughly dry) skillet over medium-high heat, shaking skillet gently in circular motion for even browning. Remove from heat.

Place another piece of nori on slatted mat. Dampen hands and spread 1 rice ball over nori. Paint strip of some of wasabi paste across middle of rice. Top with some cucumber strips and sprinkle with sesame seed. Roll up as for gourd sushi. Repeat with remaining ingredients for 4 cucumber sushi.

Cut each sushi roll into 6 pieces, wiping knife with damp towel before and after each cut. Arrange on large platter. Serve with soy sauce for dipping.

*Can be purchased at oriental markets.

**If only wasabi powder is available, mix equal parts of powder and water to form paste of appropriate consistency.

Dashi (Basic Stock)

Makes about 1 quart

5 to 6 inches dashi-konbu (dried kelp)
4½ cups cold water
⅓ cup loosely packed katsuo bushi (dried bonito flakes)

Bring kelp and water to boil in large saucepan over high heat. Immediately remove from heat and sprinkle with dried bonito flakes. Let flakes settle to bottom of saucepan (stir if they do not readily settle). Line colander with linen napkin, towel or handkerchief and set over bowl. Strain stock through cloth, twisting and squeezing to release all liquid. *(Dashi can be prepared ahead and refrigerated up to 4 days. It should not be frozen.)*

Marinated and Pickled Vegetables

Zucchini Pickles

Makes 4 half-pint jars

2 cups water
1¼ cups sugar
1 cup vinegar
1 teaspoon turmeric
1 teaspoon salt

1 teaspoon dry mustard
4 large unpeeled zucchini, thinly sliced
1 small onion, sliced
1 whole pimiento, sliced

Prepare jars. Combine first 6 ingredients in large saucepan and bring to boil. Add remaining ingredients and let boil 10 minutes. Pack into hot sterilized jars and process 10 minutes in boiling water bath. Remove from water and let cool. Test for seal. Store in cool dark place. Refrigerate after opening.

Four cucumbers, peeled and thinly sliced, can be substituted for zucchini.

Japanese Sweet Pickle Slices

Makes 4 to 5 pints

4 pounds firm young cucumbers
6 cups distilled white vinegar
3½ cups sugar
3 tablespoons mustard seed
3 tablespoons coarse salt

1 tablespoon celery seed
1 tablespoon whole allspice
1 tablespoon pickling spice

Thinly slice unpeeled cucumbers (you will have approximately 4 quarts); set aside. Combine 4 cups vinegar, ½ cup sugar, mustard seed and salt in large kettle. Bring to boil over medium-high heat, stirring to dissolve sugar. Add cucumber slices. Return to boil for 15 minutes, stirring frequently. Transfer to colander and drain well, discarding cooking liquid. Let cool slightly.

Combine remaining vinegar and sugar with celery seed, allspice and pickling spice in same kettle. Bring to boil over medium-high heat, stirring to dissolve sugar. Pack cucumbers into sterilized jars. Pour hot liquid over cucumbers, covering completely. Seal and process in boiling water bath for 5 minutes.

Pickled Dilled Green Beans

Makes 4 pints

2½ pounds green beans
Boiling water
1 bunch fresh dillweed, stems trimmed
2½ cups white vinegar

2½ cups water
¼ cup coarse salt
4 garlic cloves
1 teaspoon ground red pepper

Prepare jars. Cut beans into lengths to fit jars upright. Transfer to medium saucepan, cover with boiling water and cook over medium-high heat 3 minutes. Drain well. Pack tightly into hot sterilized jars. Divide dillweed among jars.

Combine remaining ingredients in medium saucepan and bring to boil over medium-high heat. Pour into jars to within ½ inch of top. Seal and process 10 minutes in boiling water bath. Remove from water and let cool completely. Test for seal. Store in cool dark place. Refrigerate after opening.

Dilled Mushrooms

6 servings

½ pound sliced fresh mushrooms
1 teaspoon butter or margarine
Salt and freshly ground pepper

¼ cup vinaigrette
½ bunch fresh dillweed, chopped

Lightly sauté mushrooms in butter. Do not brown. Season with salt and pepper to taste and drain.

Mix with remaining ingredients and marinate overnight or longer in refrigerator. Serve cold.

Marinated Cauliflower

6 servings

1 large head cauliflower, trimmed
Salt

2 garlic cloves, finely minced
6 tablespoons olive oil

2 tablespoons dry white Rioja wine
1 tablespoon lemon juice
Paprika

Soak cauliflower in salted water to cover for about 1 hour. Break into florets. Drop into boiling water and cook until stems are crisp-tender. Plunge into cold water to cool. Drain well.

Sauté garlic in olive oil until golden. Pour over cauliflower, then sprinkle with wine and lemon juice. Add salt to taste, mix well and dust with paprika. Marinate at least 1 hour before serving.

Pickled Cherries

Excellent served with pâté. Use as you would cornichons.

Makes about 4 quarts

5 pounds fresh cherries, stems removed
1 pound sugar

2 quarts good quality red wine vinegar
4 cinnamon sticks

Pack cherries in sterilized jars. Combine sugar, vinegar and cinnamon in 3-quart saucepan and bring to boil over medium-high heat, stirring frequently. Cook 5 minutes. Place cinnamon stick in each jar, pour syrup over and seal.

May be stored in large plastic container or jar in refrigerator for 1 year.

Spiced Olives

6 servings

2 8-ounce jars green olives
1 3-ounce jar pimientos

2 large garlic cloves
2 large fresh mint leaves or ½ teaspoon dried
1 teaspoon thyme
½ cup dry white Rioja wine

1 bay leaf
1 teaspoon dried parsley
½ teaspoon paprika
2 tablespoons lemon juice

Press olives with mallet or rolling pin so they split on 1 side. Transfer to jar and add pimientos.

Place remaining ingredients in blender and whirl until smooth. Pour over olives and pimientos, cover and refrigerate. Serve well chilled.

May be stored in refrigerator for at least 1 week.

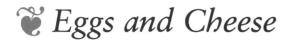 Eggs and Cheese

Tuna-Stuffed Eggs

Cooked crabmeat, chicken or any fish can be substituted for the tuna.

6 servings

¼ cup (½ stick) unsalted butter
¼ teaspoon finely chopped garlic
6 hard-cooked eggs
⅔ cup drained, flaked water-packed tuna
2½ tablespoons chopped fresh chives
Generous pinch of ground red pepper

Herb or vegetable salt
Capers, fresh dillweed sprigs, toasted slivered almonds, thinly sliced pimiento or paprika (garnish)

Beat butter and garlic in processor until light and creamy. Cut eggs in half; set whites aside. Add yolks to butter and blend well. Add tuna, chives and ground red pepper. Season with herb salt to taste. Blend until smooth. Spoon mixture into pastry bag fitted with star tip and pipe into reserved egg whites, or carefully mound mixture into whites using small spatula or spoon. Garnish as desired.
Tuna-Stuffed Eggs can be covered with plastic wrap and refrigerated 3 days.

Watercress-Stuffed Eggs

6 servings

¼ cup (½ stick) unsalted butter
6 hard-cooked eggs
2½ teaspoons finely chopped shallot
1½ teaspoons fresh lemon juice
1 cup chopped watercress, rinsed and patted dry

Generous pinch of ground red pepper
Herb or vegetable salt
Thinly sliced ripe olives or pimientos (garnish)

Beat butter in processor until light and creamy. Cut eggs in half; set whites aside. Add yolks, shallot and lemon juice to butter and blend well. Add watercress and ground red pepper. Season with herb salt to taste. Blend until watercress is just incorporated; do not overmix. Spoon mixture into pastry bag fitted with star tip and pipe into reserved egg whites, or carefully mound mixture into whites using small spatula or spoon. Garnish with sliced olives or pimientos.
Eggs can be covered with plastic wrap and refrigerated 3 days.

Smoked Turkey-Stuffed Eggs

4 to 6 servings

8 hard-cooked eggs, shelled and halved lengthwise
4 ounces ground smoked turkey
⅛ teaspoon dried sage

Bottled creamy French dressing
Minced fresh parsley

Remove yolks carefully and turn into medium bowl. Mash with fork to crumble. Stir in turkey and sage. Blend in enough dressing to moisten. Spoon mixture into egg halves. Arrange on serving platter. Garnish with parsley. Cover and chill until ready to serve.

Belgian Endive with Bleu Cheese

Prepare this delightful hors d'oeuvre a day ahead and refrigerate.

24 appetizers

3 ounces cream cheese, room temperature

3 ounces good quality bleu cheese, room temperature

2 or 3 tablespoons unsalted butter, room temperature

¼ cup (or more) whipping cream

2 large bunches Belgian endive, leaves separated, washed and drained
Paprika (garnish)

Combine cheeses, butter and ¼ cup whipping cream in processor or blender and mix until creamy, adding more cream as necessary.

Spoon mixture into pastry bag fitted with star tip and pipe into endive leaves. Arrange leaves in spoke pattern on large platter and sprinkle with paprika. Refrigerate until ready to serve.

Grapes Stuffed with Bleu Cheese

40 appetizers

½ pound large white seedless grapes

2 tablespoons unsalted butter, chilled

¼ pound bleu cheese, crumbled

Fresh grape or lemon leaves, rinsed and dried (optional garnish)

Cut each grape ¾ through from stem end. Pat grapes dry with paper towels.

Beat butter in processor or small bowl of electric mixer until creamy. Add cheese and beat until thoroughly blended. Spoon mixture into pastry bag fitted with small star tip and refrigerate until firm. Pipe some of mixture into center of grape, carefully pressing sides together. Gently transfer to tray. Repeat with remaining grapes. Chill until firm.

Just before serving, arrange grape or lemon leaves on platter and top with stuffed grapes.

Grapes can be prepared 1 day ahead.

Spiced Cheese-Stuffed Pepper Rings

A refreshing hors d'oeuvre that can be prepared a day ahead.

8 to 10 servings

1 pound cream cheese, room temperature

4 ounces shredded Gruyère cheese

¼ cup (½ stick) unsalted butter, room temperature

1 tablespoon Dijon mustard

2 to 3 teaspoons imported sweet Hungarian paprika

12 slices spicy Italian salami, chopped

6 green onions, minced
Salt and freshly ground pepper

3 *each* red and green bell peppers, stemmed, deveined and seeded

Fresh spinach or lettuce leaves (garnish)

Combine cream cheese, Gruyère, butter, mustard and paprika in processor and mix until smooth. Turn into medium bowl. Add salami and green onion, mixing until well blended. Season with salt and pepper to taste. Stuff peppers with cheese mixture, packing down with back of spoon. Chill for several hours or overnight.

To serve, arrange spinach or lettuce leaves on platter. Thinly slice peppers and arrange in fan pattern over leaves, alternating red peppers with green.

Mini Cheese Balls

Makes about 3 cups

2 cups shredded cheddar cheese
1 8-ounce package cream cheese, room temperature
1 teaspoon dry mustard

1 teaspoon Worcestershire sauce
¼ teaspoon ground red pepper
¼ cup toasted sesame seed
Assorted crackers

Combine first 5 ingredients in medium bowl and blend well. Shape mixture into small balls or roll into cylinder. Coat with sesame seed. Cover with foil or plastic wrap and chill. Serve with crackers.

Mini-Crepes with Asparagus

6 servings

6 large crepes (about 9 inches in diameter)

1 9-ounce package frozen asparagus spears

1 5-ounce package herbed cheese (room temperature)

Make 3 small crepes from each large one, using round cookie cutter.

Cook asparagus spears until crisp-tender. Cut off tips of spears so that each will be about ½ inch longer than the diameter of each little crepe.

Spread each crepe with cheese, place asparagus tip in center and roll up. Serve at room temperature or cold.

 *Seafood*

Smoked Salmon Rolls

6 servings

1 8-ounce package cream cheese, room temperature
3 tablespoons sour cream

1 2-ounce jar red caviar
½ pound thinly sliced smoked salmon

Blend cream cheese with sour cream. Gently fold in caviar and spread salmon slices with mixture. Roll up and cut into 1½-inch lengths. Serve chilled.

Herring-Stuffed Beets

6 servings

24 small whole cooked beets
1 6-ounce jar pickled herring tidbits

¼ cup sour cream
Dillweed sprigs (garnish)

With small melon scoop, hollow out top of each beet. Drain and coarsely shred herring and fill each beet with ½ teaspoon. Dot with sour cream and garnish with dillweed sprigs. Serve cold.

 *Meats*

Chinese Beef Jerky

36 appetizers

3 pounds flank steak or London broil

Marinade
½ cup light soy sauce
4½ tablespoons honey
4½ tablespoons dry Sherry

4 large garlic cloves, minced
1½ tablespoons minced fresh ginger
1½ tablespoons sesame oil
1½ tablespoons crushed red pepper
Dash of freshly ground white pepper

Cut meat in half lengthwise and slice diagonally crosswise into paper-thin strips 1½ to 2 inches wide and 4 inches long. Transfer to shallow pan. Combine marinade ingredients and rub thoroughly into meat. Arrange meat on racks and let dry at cool room temperature overnight (do not refrigerate).

Preheat oven to 250°F. Line 2 large baking sheets with foil and set wire racks on top of each. Arrange meat on racks in single layer. Bake 30 minutes.

Reduce oven temperature to 200°F, turn meat over and bake 30 minutes.

Reduce heat to 175°F and continue drying meat another 40 minutes (meat should be lightly browned but not burned). Let meat continue to dry on racks at cool room temperature overnight before packing into jars.

Dried meat can be brushed lightly with sesame oil for additional flavor and shinier appearance.

Ham-Stuffed Mushrooms

4 to 6 servings

1 cup finely chopped cooked ham
1 generous tablespoon Dijon mustard
1 tablespoon Major Grey's Chutney, minced
1 teaspoon vinegar

2 green onions, minced
Sour cream and mayonnaise (to bind)
14 (about) small to medium mushrooms, stemmed

Combine all ingredients except mushrooms. Mound in mushroom caps and chill until ready to serve. *(Can be prepared several hours ahead.)*

 *Nuts*

Holiday Roasted Nut Mix

Makes about 6 cups

1¼ pounds shelled walnuts
½ pound shelled almonds
½ pound shelled pecans
¼ pound shelled sunflower seeds

¼ pound pepitas (pumpkin seeds)
¼ pound shelled raw cashews
½ pound raisins

Preheat oven to 350°F. Combine walnuts, almonds, pecans, sunflower seeds, pepitas and cashews in large roasting pan. Roast, stirring occasionally, until nuts are golden, about 20 minutes. Let cool. Add raisins and toss well. Store mixture in airtight containers.

Fried Walnuts

Makes 1½ cups

2 cups boiling water
1½ cups walnut halves or large pieces
½ cup sugar

1 cup oil

Pour boiling water over nuts and let stand 2 to 3 minutes. Drain well. Transfer to baking sheet. Sprinkle with sugar and mix well. Spread in single layer and let stand overnight to dry.

Heat oil in wok or skillet until very hot. Add nuts in small batches and fry until golden brown, 1 to 2 minutes; *watch carefully because they can burn quickly.* Drain on rack. Store in tightly covered container in cool dry place.

Oil can be strained and used several more times for this recipe.

4 ❧ Pastries, Canapés and Breads

For the cook who enjoys baking, appetizers open up a whole world of creative possibilities. Tartlets, quiches, savory strudels, little pizzas and sandwiches, canapés, croustades, crackers, chips, pretzels—it would take pages simply to list the different kinds of first-course treats based on some variety of pastry or bread, much less the variations on each type.

Pastries are endlessly adaptable as appetizers. You can prepare a large batch of tartlet shells, for example, and freeze them before baking. Before a meal or a party, they can then be popped into the oven and filled with whatever you like: a savory mousse, a mixture of scrambled eggs and herbs, a seasoned vegetable puree, or a smooth and tangy cheese mixture such as the almond-studded cream cheese filling on page 60. Puff pastry, generally regarded as a foundation for desserts, makes excellent appetizers when combined with savory ingredients such as the mixture of cheese rolled up in Puff Pastry Palm Leaves (page 62). And tissue-thin strudel and phyllo doughs are ideal wrappers for any number of light pastry hors d'oeuvres. By following a few simple guidelines (see boxes, pages 65 and 67), you will find fragile phyllo dough easy to handle.

The humble loaf of bread can be transformed into all manner of appetizers. Sliced and toasted until "crusty," it becomes the basis of what the French call *croustades,* the Italians *crostini*—topped with elaborate combinations of cheeses, vegetables, seafoods and meats (recipes, pages 70–72). Just thinly sliced and cut into neat, crustless rounds or squares, bread can be topped with seasoned butters and cheese spreads, mousses, pâtés, cold meats or cheeses to make an array of canapés that are perfect for an appetizer buffet (see box, page 69). And, of course, there is the simple crustless "tea sandwich," cut into triangles or strips. The Watercress Sandwich (page 72) is a classic Victorian example. A character in Oscar Wilde's *The Importance of Being Earnest* consumes a whole plate of these tidbits, on stage. No doubt your guests will do likewise—and in this case the applause will be all yours.

 Pastries

Filled Tartlets

28 appetizers

2 cups milk
3 beaten eggs
½ cup grated Swiss cheese
Dash of nutmeg
Salt and freshly ground white pepper

2 strips cooked bacon, crumbled
1 6-ounce can shredded crabmeat, shell and cartilage removed

28 Tartlet Shells (see following recipe)

Scald milk. Remove from heat and let cool. Stir in eggs, cheese and seasoning.

Divide mixture between two bowls. Add bacon to one mixture, crabmeat to the other.

Preheat oven to 400°F. Arrange Tartlet Shells on greased baking sheet. Fill 14 shells with bacon mixture, 14 with crabmeat mixture. Bake for 15 minutes. Serve warm.

Tartlet Shells

This is a firm crust that will hold liquid-type fillings without breaking or falling apart. Do not double recipe. Make two separate batches of 14 shells each.

14 tartlet shells

2 cups all purpose flour
½ teaspoon salt
1 stick butter
½ cup ice water (or less)

1 egg white beaten with 1 teaspoon water

Preheat oven to 450°F. Blend flour, salt and butter until mixture resembles cornmeal. Add just enough water to shape dough into ball.

Roll pastry ⅛ inch thick. Cut out pieces to fit into 3-inch tartlet tins. Place pastry in buttered tins. Cover with circles of waxed paper or foil and fill with dried peas or beans. Arrange tins on baking sheet. Bake 10 to 12 minutes. Remove paper and beans. Return to oven 2 or 3 minutes more. Turn off heat. Brush inside of tarts with egg white mixture. Keep tarts in oven with door open 1 to 2 minutes to dry thoroughly. Unmold and fill.

Cream Cheese and Almond Tartlets

36 to 48 appetizers

¼ cup (½ stick) unsalted butter, room temperature
¼ pound cream cheese, room temperature
¼ teaspoon curry powder
Hot pepper sauce

36 to 48 baked Cheese Whole Wheat Short Pastry Tartlet Shells (see following recipe)
¼ cup finely chopped toasted blanched almonds

Beat butter in large bowl of electric mixer until creamy. Add cream cheese and beat again. Blend in curry powder and hot pepper sauce. Fill pastry shells with mixture. Sprinkle with nuts.

Cheese Whole Wheat Short Pastry Tartlet Shells

36 to 48 tartlet shells

2 cups whole wheat pastry flour
½ cup freshly grated Parmesan cheese
1 teaspoon dry mustard
1 teaspoon sweet paprika
⅛ teaspoon ground red pepper
½ cup plus 2 tablespoons (1¼ sticks) cold unsalted butter, cut into ½-inch pieces

1 egg yolk mixed with ice water to equal ¼ cup
Ice water (optional)

Additional whole wheat pastry flour

Combine flour, cheese, dry mustard, paprika and ground red pepper in large mixing bowl. Add butter and blend with fingertips until mixture resembles coarse meal. Add egg yolk and water mixture and blend well, working dough as little as possible and adding more water 1 tablespoon at a time if dough is too dry. Turn dough out onto unfloured work surface and quickly form into ball. Cover with plastic wrap and refrigerate 30 minutes.

Arrange tartlet tins on baking sheet with sides touching. Cut 2 pieces of waxed paper 24 inches long. Place 1 sheet on work surface and dust with additional flour. Set dough in center of paper and sprinkle with flour. Flatten dough with rolling pin and cover with remaining waxed paper. Roll dough out to thickness of ⅛ inch. Remove top sheet of waxed paper. Lifting bottom sheet, invert dough over tartlet tins. Press dough firmly against sides and bottoms. Run rolling pin over top to trim off excess dough. Prick bottoms with fork. Line pastries with waxed paper and fill with dried beans or rice. Bake in 350°F oven 10 to 15 minutes, depending on size of tins. Discard paper and beans or rice. Continue baking until bottoms are browned, about 3 to 4 minutes. Fill as desired.

Filled Barquettes

8 to 10 servings

36 2-inch-long baked barquettes*
1 12-ounce package frozen spinach soufflé, thawed

Freshly grated Parmesan cheese

Preheat oven to 400°F. Spoon thawed spinach soufflé into barquettes and bake on greased baking sheets until golden (about 10 minutes). Sprinkle with Parmesan. Serve hot.

*Barquettes may be prepared ahead of time from your favorite recipe or purchased from a bakery.

Curried Chicken Pufflets

36 appetizers

36 miniature cream puffs*
1 10½-ounce can cream of chicken soup
1 tablespoon curry powder

1½ cups chopped cooked chicken
Salt and freshly ground pepper
Paprika (garnish)

Split each cream puff in half. Combine undiluted soup, curry powder and chopped chicken and heat through over low heat. Season to taste with salt and pepper. Fill bottoms of puffs with the hot mixture and replace tops. Serve at once sprinkled with paprika, if desired.

*Purchase cream puffs at bakery or use a favorite cream puff recipe.

Puff Pastry Palm Leaves with Cheese

24 appetizers

½ pound Whole Wheat Puff Pastry (see following recipe)

1 cup freshly grated Parmesan cheese

1 cup freshly grated Gruyère cheese
Ground red pepper

1 egg, beaten

Turn dough out onto lightly floured surface and roll into rectangle ⅛ inch thick. Brush dough with water. Cover evenly with ¾ cup Parmesan and ¾ cup Gruyère. Sprinkle lightly with ground red pepper. Roll one long side of dough tightly to center. Roll up remaining side to meet at center. Invert dough and cut into slices ½ inch thick. Transfer to dampened baking sheet. Flatten each slice slightly. Freeze 30 minutes.

Preheat oven to 400°F. Bake 15 minutes. Turn "palm leaves" over and brush with egg. Sprinkle with remaining cheese and continue baking until cheese is melted and lightly browned, about 5 to 10 minutes.

Pastry can be filled and rolled ahead and refrigerated. Cut just before baking. Baked palm leaves can be frozen. Reheat in 300°F oven for 10 minutes.

Whole Wheat Puff Pastry

Makes 1 pound

2 cups stone-ground whole wheat bread flour

½ teaspoon sea salt

⅓ cup plus 2 tablespoons ice-cold water or well-chilled nonfat milk

2 teaspoons fresh lemon juice

1¼ cups (2½ sticks) unsalted butter, chilled and cut into ½-inch cubes

Combine 1¾ cups flour and salt in processor and mix using 1 to 2 on/off turns. With machine running, add water or milk and lemon juice and mix until dough forms ball, about 2 to 3 minutes. Turn dough out onto *unfloured* surface and shape into smooth ball. Make deep crosscut on top of ball using sharp knife. Cover with plastic wrap and chill in freezer until firm, about 30 minutes.

Meanwhile, combine butter and remaining flour in large bowl and mix until smooth. Turn out onto surface. Form into 4-inch square using spatula. Cover butter with plastic wrap and chill in freezer until firm, about 20 minutes.

When dough and butter are chilled to equal firmness, but not frozen, transfer dough to lightly floured surface and roll into 12-inch square. Set butter mixture in center of dough and fold sides over butter evenly, making sure ends meet in center. Pinch ends of dough together so there are no holes. Using rolling pin, make series of slight depressions in crisscross pattern over dough until square is flattened to 8 inches. Roll dough into rectangle. Fold top ⅓ toward center; fold remaining ⅓ over top, as for business letter. *This is called a single turn.* Cover with plastic wrap and chill in freezer until firm, but not frozen, about 20 minutes.

Turn dough out onto lightly floured surface with open end toward you. Roll into large rectangle about ⅜ inch thick. Fold short ends so they meet at center of dough without overlapping. Fold dough in half at center. *This is called a double turn.* Cover with plastic wrap and chill in freezer until firm, but not frozen, about 20 minutes.

Repeat single turn, chilling in freezer until firm but not frozen, about 20 minutes. Repeat double turn 3 more times, chilling in freezer after each. Cover with plastic wrap and refrigerate.

Whole Wheat Puff Pastry can be frozen but is best when prepared and baked the same day.

Anchovy Puffs

60 appetizers

1 3-ounce package cream cheese, room temperature
½ cup (1 stick) unsalted butter, room temperature

1 cup all purpose flour
1 2-ounce tube anchovy paste

Beat cheese with butter until well blended. Add flour and mix thoroughly. Transfer dough to plastic bag and flatten into disc. Chill.

Preheat oven to 400°F. Roll dough out on lightly floured surface to thickness of about ⅛ inch. Cut into 2-inch rounds using cookie or biscuit cutter. Spread each with anchovy paste. Fold over and crimp edges with fork. Transfer to baking sheet and bake until lightly golden, about 8 to 10 minutes.

Hot Mushroom-Filled Cheese Puffs

36 appetizers

Cheese Puffs
1 cup all purpose flour
⅛ teaspoon freshly ground pepper
Dash of ground red pepper
Dash of nutmeg
1 cup water
6 tablespoons (¾ stick) unsalted butter
1 teaspoon salt
8 dashes red pepper sauce
4 eggs
½ cup freshly grated Parmesan cheese

Mushroom Filling
2 pounds mushrooms, trimmed, well cleaned and dried
6 tablespoons (¾ stick) butter
½ cup minced shallot or green onion
⅛ teaspoon freshly grated nutmeg
Salt and freshly ground pepper

1 pound whipped cream cheese

For cheese puffs: Preheat oven to 425°F. Grease baking sheets and set aside.

Combine flour, peppers and nutmeg in small bowl. Mix water, butter and salt in heavy medium saucepan. Bring to boil, stirring occasionally until butter is melted. Reduce heat, add flour mixture all at once and stir vigorously until mixture is smooth and pulls away from sides of pan. Remove from heat and allow to cool for 5 minutes.

Using electric hand mixer (or processor), beat red pepper sauce into batter. Add eggs one at a time, beating well after each addition until mixture is smooth and shiny. Beat in cheese.

Fit pastry bag with ½-inch round tip and fill with dough. Squeeze onto baking sheet in 1-inch mounds. Bake until puffed and golden, about 20 minutes. Turn off oven. Remove baking sheet and slit side of each puff with sharp knife. Return to oven, leaving door ajar, until puffs are dry, about 10 minutes. Let cool on racks in draft-free area.

For filling: Chop mushrooms in processor. Melt butter in heavy skillet over medium-high heat. Add shallot and mushrooms and cook until pieces begin to dry and separate; *watch carefully to avoid burning.* Reduce heat and continue cooking until browned. Season with nutmeg and salt and pepper to taste. Allow filling to cool.

To serve: Preheat oven to 300°F. Slice off tops from puffs. Combine cream cheese and mushroom filling and blend well *(do not beat)*. Divide among puffs, replacing tops. Bake 5 minutes. Serve hot.

Kreatopetes (Spicy Meat-Stuffed Appetizers)

These wine-scented turn-overs can be assembled up to six months ahead and frozen. To bake directly from freezer, brush unthawed triangles with melted butter before cooking. Increase baking time by about 20 minutes.

36 appetizers

2 tablespoons (¼ stick) unsalted butter
5 green onions, chopped
5 garlic cloves, minced
1¼ pounds freshly ground meat (lean beef or lamb, turkey or pork sausage, alone or in combination)
⅔ cup red wine
½ cup minced fresh parsley
½ cup canned tomato sauce
1 tablespoon dried oregano, crumbled
1 tablespoon dried basil, crumbled
2 teaspoons dried rosemary, crumbled

½ teaspoon chili powder
1 teaspoon curry powder
½ medium onion, chopped
⅓ cup freshly grated Parmesan cheese
1 egg, lightly beaten
12 phyllo pastry sheets (about ½ pound)

½ cup (1 stick) unsalted butter, melted with ½ cup olive oil

Sesame seed

Melt 2 tablespoons butter in large skillet over medium heat. Add half of chopped green onion and half of minced garlic and sauté 3 to 4 minutes. Stir in ground meat and cook until no longer pink. Pour in all but 2 tablespoons wine and simmer 2 to 3 minutes. Reduce heat to medium-low, add ¼ cup parsley, tomato sauce, oregano, basil, rosemary and chili powder and simmer 15 minutes.

Drain any fat from meat. Blend in remaining green onion, garlic, parsley and red wine. Stir in curry powder and chopped onion. Let cool. Mix in Parmesan and beaten egg. Set aside.

Stack phyllo on work surface. Cut lengthwise into thirds; stack again. Cover phyllo with waxed paper and damp towel to prevent drying.

Remove top strip of phyllo and brush with butter mixture. With short end in front of you, fold long sides into center to form strip approximately 11 × 2 inches. Place 1 teaspoon meat filling at bottom end. Fold pastry strip up over filling so bottom edge meets left edge, forming a triangle. Continue folding back at right angles to make triangular shape, tucking in any remaining phyllo at end. Repeat procedure with remaining phyllo and filling.

Preheat oven to 350°F. Generously butter baking sheet. Arrange phyllo triangles on sheet. Brush generously with butter mixture and sprinkle with sesame seed. Bake triangles 1 sheet at a time, brushing once with butter mixture halfway through baking time, until crisp and golden, 25 to 30 minutes. Transfer to large platter. Serve hot.

Spinach Feta Strudel Slices

This wonderful appetizer is also a winner as a main course for luncheons or light suppers, or as a unique vegetable side dish on a buffet table.

42 servings

2 pounds fresh spinach, including stems
¼ cup (½ stick) butter
12 green onions, white part only, minced (½ cup)

6 ounces chilled feta cheese, coarsely chopped (1½ cups)
½ cup fresh breadcrumbs

½ cup parsley leaves, minced
4 egg whites
4 tablespoons fresh dillweed or 2 tablespoons dried
Salt and freshly ground pepper

¾ pound phyllo pastry sheets
1 cup (2 sticks) unsalted butter, melted

Wash spinach; cut off root ends. Cook spinach quickly in uncovered pot only in water clinging to leaves, turning twice to promote even cooking. As soon as

> ### 🍎 *Buying and Storing Phyllo Dough*
>
> Excellent packaged phyllo is available in stores—and a good thing, too, because making the sheets from scratch is a difficult proposition even for advanced pastry cooks. Fresh phyllo can be found in Greek and Armenian markets, and many supermarkets carry the frozen variety. The commercial phyllo labeled "thin," which has about 25 sheets to a package, is preferable for home use to the kind labeled "ultra-thin." Before purchasing, it is important to look at the edges of the phyllo sheets: Torn or crumbling edges are a sign of improper handling or storage.
>
> Despite its fragile appearance, phyllo is actually quite strong if not allowed to dry out. It should be covered with waxed paper and a damp towel until you are ready to butter and fill it. If using frozen phyllo, do not defrost at room temperature. This will make the outside sheets sticky and leave the inner ones still unthawed. For best results, place the phyllo in the refrigerator for five hours or overnight.

spinach wilts, transfer to colander and run under cold water until spinach is cool to the touch. Drain well. Place in corner of kitchen towel and wring out all moisture. Transfer to processor or blender and puree.

Melt ¼ cup butter in small skillet. Add onion and sauté 5 minutes.

Using electric mixer or processor, combine spinach puree, onion, feta cheese, 2 tablespoons breadcrumbs, parsley, egg whites, dillweed, salt and pepper and blend well. Taste for seasoning (mixture should be highly seasoned).

Preheat oven to 375°F. Generously butter baking sheet. Place 1 phyllo sheet lengthwise in front of you on waxed paper set on damp towel. Cover remaining sheets with waxed paper and wrap in another damp towel. Brush phyllo with some of the melted butter and sprinkle with 1 teaspoon remaining breadcrumbs. Repeat buttering and crumbing process using 3 additional phyllo sheets.

Spread ⅓ of spinach mixture on phyllo ¼ inch from long edge closest to you. Roll tightly and firmly (like a jelly roll) using waxed paper to assist. Transfer to prepared baking sheet. Brush top lightly with some of remaining melted butter. Repeat twice for a total of 3 strudel rolls. Bake until golden brown, about 30 to 35 minutes. Cut into 1-inch slices using electric or serrated knife.

If using frozen phyllo, thaw in refrigerator overnight before preparing strudel.

Tyropetes (Fennel-Spiced Cheese Triangles)

Can be assembled up to two days ahead and refrigerated, or frozen for several months. From freezer, brush unthawed triangles with melted butter; bake 15 minutes longer.

36 appetizers

4 green onions, finely chopped
5 ounces cream cheese, room temperature
5 ounces ricotta or farmer's cheese
1 cup crumbled feta cheese, rinsed
½ cup grated Gruyère cheese
3 tablespoons minced fresh parsley
2 teaspoons fennel seed
1 egg, well beaten

12 phyllo pastry sheets (about ½ pound)

½ cup (1 stick) unsalted butter, melted with ½ cup olive oil

Sesame seed

Combine onion, all cheeses, parsley and fennel seed in medium bowl and mix well with fork. Blend in egg.

Stack phyllo on work surface. Cut lengthwise into thirds; stack again. Cover phyllo with waxed paper and damp towel to prevent drying.

Remove top strip of phyllo and brush with butter mixture. With short end in front of you, fold long sides into center to form strip approximately 11 × 2 inches. Place 1 teaspoon cheese filling at bottom end. Fold pastry strip up over filling so bottom edge meets left edge, forming a triangle. Continue folding back at right angles to make triangular shape, tucking in any remaining phyllo at end. Repeat procedure with remaining phyllo and filling.

Preheat oven to 350°F. Generously butter baking sheet. Arrange phyllo triangles on sheet. Brush generously with butter mixture and sprinkle with sesame seed. Bake triangles 1 sheet at a time, brushing once with butter mixture halfway through baking time, until crisp and golden, 25 to 30 minutes.

Lahmajoon (Armenian Pizza)

100 appetizers

Filling
- 2 pounds lean ground meat (1½ pounds beef and ½ pound lamb)
- ½ cup all purpose flour
- 1 large onion, finely chopped
- 1 green pepper, finely chopped
- ½ bunch parsley, finely chopped
- 1 14½-ounce can whole peeled tomatoes, drained and chopped
- ½ cup tomato sauce
- 6 tablespoons tomato paste
- 1 2-ounce jar diced pimientos
- 3 garlic cloves, minced
  Ground red pepper
  Salt and freshly ground pepper

Crust
- 3 1-pound loaves frozen bread dough, thawed
  Flour

For filling: Combine ground meat and flour and mix well. Add remaining ingredients and blend thoroughly.

Place 1 pound of dough on well-floured work surface. Sprinkle rolling pin and dough with flour and roll dough into large circle about ⅛ inch thick, adding flour as needed to prevent sticking.

Cut circles 3 to 4 inches in diameter using jar lid or tuna can. Place 1 tablespoon meat mixture on each circle, spreading to edges with fork to prevent burning. *(Filling will shrink a bit during cooking but, if too much is added, excess juices will cause crust to become soggy.)*

Preheat oven to 400°F. Arrange pizzas on ungreased baking sheets and bake for 15 to 20 minutes. Serve warm or at room temperature.

Pizzas can be frozen. To reheat, arrange without thawing on baking sheet, tent with foil and heat through, about 10 to 15 minutes in 375°F oven.

Pizzas can be made larger and served as a luncheon or light dinner entrée with a green salad dressed with oil and vinegar.

🍎 *Folding Phyllo Triangles*

- Place 6 sheets of phyllo pastry on a flat surface, one on top of the other. Recover the remaining pastry with waxed paper and a damp towel. Refrigerate until needed. Cut the stack of 6 sheets of pastry into strips approximately 3 inches wide, or the size your recipe specifies. Remove 6 strips, stack the remaining strips, cover with waxed paper and damp towel until needed.

- Place the 6 strips side by side on flat surface. Brush with butter quickly; dust lightly with breadcrumbs. Fold each strip in half from top to bottom.

- Place about 1 teaspoon of filling on the bottom end of pastry strip— end nearest you (Figure 1).

- Fold the pastry strip back over the filling so the bottom edge meets the left edge, forming a right angle (Figure 2).

- Continue folding back at right angles to make the triangular shape, tucking in any remaining phyllo at the end (Figures 3, 4 and 5).

- Brush generously with butter, place on baking sheet and refrigerate or freeze. When pastry is chilled and firm, cover with plastic wrap or layer in cardboard boxes. Wrap in freezerproof paper or foil and freeze. Bake in 350°F oven until golden and crisp, turning once; if frozen, defrost 30 minutes before baking.

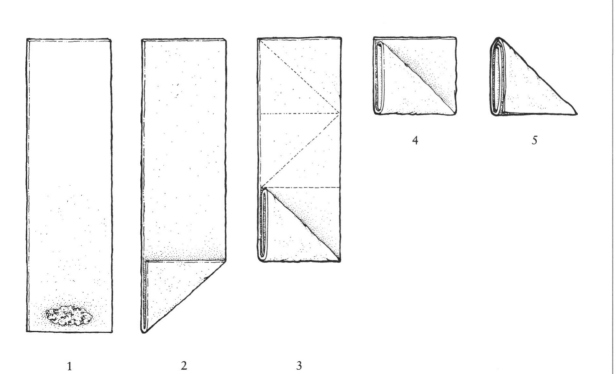

1   2   3   4   5

Slovenian Mushroom Pastries

54 to 60 appetizers

2½ cups all purpose flour
⅔ cup butter, room temperature
8 tablespoons sour cream
2 eggs

2 tablespoons olive oil

1 onion, finely minced
½ pound mushrooms, finely chopped
Salt and freshly ground pepper
Dash of dried tarragon

Combine flour, butter, 6 tablespoons sour cream and 1 egg to make soft dough. Cover with plastic.

Meanwhile, heat oil in large skillet over low heat. Add onion and cook until it just begins to become translucent. Add mushrooms and continue cooking about 5 minutes. Remove from heat. Blend in remaining sour cream, salt, pepper and tarragon. Let cool.

Preheat oven to 475°F. Lightly oil baking sheets. Roll out pastry on lightly floured surface to thickness of slightly less than ¼ inch. Cut dough into 2-inch squares. Place about 1 teaspoon mushroom mixture in each.

Beat remaining egg and use to brush edges of squares lightly. Fold corners of pastry toward center, overlapping and pressing edges together to seal. Brush tops with egg. Transfer to baking sheets.

Lightly dust packets with pepper. Bake until golden brown, about 15 minutes (tops will pop open a bit). *Do not open oven during first 7 minutes of baking time or pastry will fall.* Serve either warm or at room temperature.

Canapés, Croustades and Sandwiches

Mozzarella-Tomato Canapés

12 appetizers

12 thin 2 × 2-inch slices part-skim mozzarella cheese
12 2 × 2-inch whole wheat crackers
2 tablespoons finely chopped fresh basil or oregano or 1 tablespoon dried oregano, crumbled

12 thin tomato slices

Place mozzarella slice on cracker. Sprinkle with some of chopped basil and top with tomato slice. Repeat with remaining crackers. Arrange on serving platter. Serve at room temperature.

Curried Chicken-Almond Canapés

60 to 72 appetizers

1 cup minced, cooked chicken*
1 cup mayonnaise
¾ cup shredded Monterey Jack cheese (3 ounces)
⅓ cup ground almonds
¼ cup parsley leaves, minced
2 large shallots, minced
2 teaspoons fresh lemon juice

1½ teaspoons curry powder or to taste
Dash of hot pepper sauce
Salt and freshly ground pepper

60 to 72 1½-inch rounds of thinly sliced bread
60 to 72 almond slices

🍎 A Canapé Primer

These open-face or tea-size sandwiches are best assembled just before guests arrive. Otherwise they become soggy. Choose a fresh unsliced *pain de mie*-style loaf (rectangular with a flat top). Remove the crust. Slice bread ¼ inch thick (thinner for closed sandwiches). Much of the preparation can be done ahead: Slice bread early in the day, wrap tightly and store at room temperature. Prepare any fillings or garnishes ahead and refrigerate, but bring spreads to room temperature before using so bread does not tear. Cover slices completely with topping and divide into squares, rectangles or other interesting shapes with a knife or special cutters. Garnish as desired. If serving canapés hot, you can prepare several hours ahead by toasting both sides of bread, spreading with topping and cutting out shapes. Heat in 200°F oven briefly before serving.

Some possibilities for cold canapé toppings are roast beef with a rosette of horseradish cream garnished with a cornichon "fan"; a smoked salmon and cream cheese spread with capers garnished with a sprig of dill; anchovy butter decorated with roasted red pepper strips and a rolled anchovy; shrimp with watercress mayonnaise; and Italian salami with mustard-basil butter.

Slicing Variations

Striped canapés: Slice four different types of bread as thin as possible, trimming as necessary so they are all the same size. Spread three of the slices with various flavored butters, cream cheese or mousseline, spreading evenly to edges. Stack them like a layer cake and top with the plain piece of bread, pressing gently so layers adhere. Cut loaf vertically into slices ¼ inch thick (and then cut into 1- or 2-inch-wide strips for easier serving if desired).

Pinwheels: For best results, flash freeze unsliced bread for 15 to 30 minutes after trimming crusts. This will make slicing easier. Thinly cut loaf *lengthwise* into as many slices as possible. Gently run a rolling pin over slices to increase their flexibility. Spread each first with butter and then with a generous amount of filling, leaving ¼-inch border on all sides. Set on length of plastic wrap, and using plastic as aid, roll up lengthwise, pressing lightly to seal. Wrap cylinder in plastic and refrigerate until filling is firm, about 30 minutes. Cut into slices ¼ inch thick for individual canapés.

Rolled canapés: For best results, flash freeze unsliced bread for 15 to 30 minutes after trimming crusts. This will make slicing easier. Thinly cut loaf vertically into as many slices as possible. Gently run a rolling pin over slices to increase their flexibility. Spread each slice first with butter and then with a generous amount of filling, leaving ¼-inch border on all sides. Roll up, pressing lightly to seal. Cut rolls in half if desired. Garnish by dipping ends in mayonnaise or softened butter and then into minced fresh herbs.

Combine all ingredients except bread and almond slices in large bowl and blend well. Cover and refrigerate.

Just before ready to serve, preheat oven to 500°F. Spread about 1½ teaspoons chicken mixture on each round, mounding in center. Top each with almond slice. Place on baking sheet and bake until lightly colored and sizzling, about 5 to 8 minutes. Serve hot.

*Crabmeat or shrimp can be substituted.

Parmesan Rounds

120 appetizers

2 loaves sliced white bread
Butter

2 8-ounce packages cream cheese, room temperature

½ cup (1 stick) butter, melted

¼ cup plus 2 tablespoons mayonnaise

6 green onions, chopped
Freshly grated Parmesan cheese

Preheat broiler. Using 1-inch round cutter, cut 3 circles from each bread slice. Butter 1 side of each circle. Arrange in single layer on baking sheet. Broil until lightly toasted. Turn and broil unbuttered side until lightly toasted. Transfer to rack and cool.

Combine cream cheese, ½ cup butter, mayonnaise and green onion in large bowl. Spread about 1 teaspoon mixture over buttered side of bread. Dip into Parmesan cheese. *(Can be prepared ahead to this point and frozen.)* Preheat broiler. Arrange rounds on baking sheet. Broil until bubbly and golden, about 5 minutes. Serve immediately.

Turkish Bread Rounds with Mediterranean Zucchini Salad

The bread rounds are best right out of the skillet, but they can be prepared ahead, wrapped in foil and reheated in a 350°F oven for 25 minutes. The salad can also be served in wedges of pita bread or with lettuce leaf "scoops."

16 servings

Turkish Bread Rounds
1 cup warm water (105°F to 115°F)
1 teaspoon yeast
1 teaspoon sugar

2½ cups unbleached all purpose flour
3 tablespoons oil
1 teaspoon salt

Mediterranean Zucchini Salad
2 small zucchini (8 ounces total), cut into 1-inch matchsticks (2 cups)
1 small green pepper (4 ounces), cut into 1-inch matchsticks (½ cup)
1 small tomato, coarsely chopped (⅓ cup)

½ cup shredded Monterey Jack or mozzarella cheese (2 ounces)
¼ cup parsley leaves, minced
4 Greek olives (preferably Kalamata), split and pitted
2 large green onions (1½ ounces total), thinly sliced
2 tablespoons fresh lemon juice
2 tablespoons oil
1½ teaspoons wine vinegar
1½ teaspoons anchovy paste
½ teaspoon dried dillweed
Pinch of dried oregano
Salt and freshly ground pepper

For bread rounds: Oil large bowl; set aside. Combine water, yeast and sugar in another mixing bowl and let proof until foamy, about 10 minutes.

Add 2 cups flour, oil and salt and blend well; add remaining flour if dough is too wet (dough should be moist). Knead into smooth ball until it leaves sides of bowl. Transfer to oiled bowl, turning to coat all surfaces. Cover with damp towel and let stand in warm place until doubled in bulk, about 1 hour.

Meanwhile, prepare zucchini salad. Combine all ingredients for salad in large bowl and toss gently but thoroughly. Taste and adjust seasoning (salad should be highly seasoned). Cover and chill until ready to use.

Place dough on well-floured board. Cut into 16 equal pieces. Roll out each piece as thinly as possible into circle 4 inches in diameter. Place each round on lightly floured baking sheet.

Heat heavy skillet over medium-high heat. Oil lightly. Place a bread round in skillet, stretching and patting into neat circle. Cook quickly on both sides until browned lightly in spots, about 30 seconds per side. *Repeat until all are cooked, making sure pan regains high heat for each piece.* Bread rounds are best served right out of the pan, but they may be stacked while still warm and wrapped in foil to retain moisture.

Drain salad; taste and adjust seasoning again. Serve from bowl beside basket of warm bread rounds. Let guests help themselves (about 2 generous tablespoons of salad will fill each round).

Crostino Caldo Alla Re Guido d'Andrea

4 appetizers

4 slices mozzarella cheese
4 teaspoons capers, rinsed, drained and minced
1 2-ounce can anchovy fillets, soaked in milk for 30 minutes to 1 hour and drained
4 small mushrooms, thinly sliced Truffles (optional)
4 teaspoons chopped fresh parsley
½ teaspoon dried basil, crumbled

4 slices Gruyère cheese
2 medium tomatoes, thinly sliced
4 tablespoons freshly grated Parmesan cheese
4 slices prosciutto
4 thin slices Italian bread, toasted Oil
Freshly ground pepper

Preheat oven to 400°F. Layer mozzarella, capers, anchovies, mushrooms, truffles, parsley, basil, Gruyère, tomatoes, Parmesan and prosciutto in equal amounts over toast. Brush lightly with oil and sprinkle with pepper. Transfer to baking sheet. Bake until cheeses have melted slightly, about 10 minutes. Serve immediately.

Crostini al Ginepro

24 appetizers

2 tablespoons olive oil
1 tablespoon unsalted butter
10 chicken livers, coarsely chopped
2 garlic cloves
4 to 5 small sage leaves
7 juniper berries
Salt and freshly ground pepper
2 cups chicken or beef broth
2 anchovy fillets, rinsed, drained and finely chopped

1 teaspoon capers packed in wine vinegar, drained and finely chopped
24 small thin slices day-old bread (toasted if desired)

Heat oil with butter in medium skillet over medium heat. Add chicken livers, garlic and sage and cook gently 10 to 15 minutes. Add juniper berries, salt and pepper and 1 cup broth. Simmer until liquid has evaporated. Remove from heat and discard juniper berries. Let cool slightly, then chop mixture finely. Return to skillet, add remaining broth and cook over medium-high heat until almost all of liquid is evaporated. Remove from heat. Using fork, add anchovies and capers and blend to paste. Taste and season with salt and pepper. Spread over bread. Transfer to platter and let stand 30 minutes before serving.

Crostini di Fegatini di Pollo

24 appetizers

2 tablespoons (¼ stick) unsalted butter
½ pound chicken livers, coarsely chopped
10 parsley sprigs (preferably Italian), finely chopped
4 fresh sage leaves, chopped

¼ cup capers, rinsed, drained and finely chopped
2 anchovy fillets, mashed with fork
1½ tablespoons red wine vinegar
1 loaf Italian or French bread, cut into 2- to 3-inch squares or rounds and toasted

Melt butter in medium saucepan over medium heat. Add livers, parsley, sage and capers. Cook just until livers are no longer pink. Add anchovies and vinegar and cook 1 to 2 minutes more. Spread on toasted bread and serve.

Mushroom-Sausage Croustades

18 appetizers

Croustades
Butter
18 slices white bread, cut into 3-inch rounds

Filling
¼ cup (½ stick) butter
3 tablespoons finely chopped shallot
½ pound mushrooms, finely chopped
2 tablespoons all purpose flour

1½ tablespoons finely chopped chives
1 tablespoon finely chopped parsley
½ teaspoon salt
Ground red pepper
¼ pound sweet Italian sausage, cut into pieces
1 cup whipping cream
½ teaspoon fresh lemon juice

2 tablespoons grated Parmesan cheese

For croustades: Preheat oven to 400°F. Butter small muffin tin. Roll each bread round out on work surface to flatten. Carefully fit bread into muffin tin, pressing gently to form cup. Bake until lightly browned, about 8 minutes. Remove from tin and let cool on wire rack. *(Croustades can be prepared ahead, sealed tightly in plastic bags and frozen.)*

For filling: Melt butter in large heavy skillet over medium-high heat. Add shallot and sauté until browned. Blend in mushrooms, stirring constantly until liquid is evaporated, 10 to 15 minutes. Sprinkle with flour, chives, parsley, salt and red pepper. Add sausage, stirring constantly until browned and crumbly. Pour in cream and bring to low boil. Reduce heat and simmer until mixture thickens, about 10 minutes. Remove from heat; stir in lemon juice. Let cool slightly.

To assemble: Preheat oven to 350°F. Spoon filling evenly into croustades. Arrange on baking sheet. Sprinkle cheese over tops. Bake until cheese melts, about 10 minutes. Serve immediately.

Watercress Sandwiches

9 to 10 servings

½ pound cream cheese, room temperature
2 bunches watercress leaves, rinsed, dried and finely chopped
Prepared horseradish

Salt
18 to 20 slices Sandwich Bread (see recipe, opposite page)

Beat cream cheese in large bowl until smooth and creamy. Add watercress and blend well. Add horseradish and salt to taste (mixture should be spicy).

Trim crusts from bread. Spread slices with cream cheese mixture, covering thinly and evenly. Cut slices into triangles or strips before serving.

Trumps Herb Butter Tea Sandwiches

10 to 12 appetizers

½ cup (1 stick) unsalted butter, room temperature
4 ounces cream cheese, room temperature
2 ounces goat cheese, room temperature

1 cup chopped fresh parsley
1 cup chopped seasonal aromatic herbs (basil, tarragon, rosemary)
Salt and freshly ground pepper
Thinly sliced bread

Combine all ingredients except bread in large bowl and blend thoroughly. Spread over half of bread slices. Close sandwiches and cut into triangles or strips.

Breads, Crackers and Chips

Sandwich Bread

4 loaves

1 cup warm water (105°F to 115°F)
1 teaspoon sugar
2 envelopes dry yeast

2 cups warm water (105°F to 115°F)

½ cup sugar
½ cup vegetable oil
1 tablespoon salt
9 cups (about) all purpose flour

Lightly grease large bowl and set aside. Combine 1 cup warm water and 1 teaspoon sugar in another large mixing bowl. Sprinkle with yeast and stir until dissolved. Let stand in warm draft-free area until foamy, about 10 minutes.

Stir in remaining water and remaining sugar with oil and salt. Beat in flour 1 cup at a time until dough begins to hold together but is still sticky. Turn dough out onto lightly floured surface and knead until smooth and elastic, adding more flour as necessary.

Form dough into ball. Transfer to lightly greased bowl, turning to coat entire surface. Cover bowl with plastic wrap, then with warm damp towel. Let stand in warm draft-free area until doubled in bulk, about 1½ hours.

Lightly grease 8 × 4-inch loaf pans. Punch dough down. Turn out onto lightly floured surface and knead briefly. Divide dough equally into fourths. Shape each into loaf and transfer to prepared pans. Cover pans with plastic wrap and then with warm damp towel. Let dough stand in warm draft-free area until doubled, about 1½ hours.

Preheat oven to 400°F. Bake until loaves are golden brown and sound hollow when tapped on bottom, about 20 minutes. Turn out onto wire racks and let cool.

Loaves can be wrapped airtight and stored in freezer up to 4 weeks.

Crusty French Bread

6 baguettes or 3 large loaves

2 envelopes dry yeast
½ cup warm water (105°F to 115°F)

7 cups unbleached all purpose flour
2¼ cups warm water (105°F to 115°F)

4 teaspoons salt

Flour

Generously grease large bowl. Lightly oil 6 baguette bread pans or 3 French bread pans. Sprinkle yeast over ½ cup warm water and stir until dissolved. Let stand until foamy, about 5 minutes.

Combine 5 cups flour and 2¼ cups warm water in another large mixing bowl. Add yeast and remaining 2 cups flour. Stir in 4 teaspoons salt.

Turn dough out onto lightly floured surface and knead until smooth and elastic, adding flour as necessary to prevent sticking, 8 to 10 minutes. Transfer dough to greased bowl, turning to coat all surfaces. Cover with plastic wrap and let stand in warm draft-free area until doubled in volume, 1 to 1½ hours.

Punch dough down. Transfer to work surface and knead gently 1 to 2 minutes. Return to greased bowl, turning to coat all surfaces. Let stand in warm draft-free area until doubled, 3 hours.

Turn dough out onto work surface. Divide into 6 or 3 equal pieces. Flatten 1 piece into rectangle. Fold long edge over ⅓; fold over remaining long edge as for business letter to form narrow rectangle. Pinch edges together to seal. Repeat with remaining dough. Roll each rectangle into 18-inch cylinder using rocking motion. Transfer to prepared pans. Cover dough and let rise until doubled, about 1½ hours.

Preheat oven to 450°F. Arrange shallow roasting pan in lower rack of oven and fill halfway with water.

Holding tip of sharp knife on the bias, make 3 diagonal slashes across top of each baguette or loaf. Transfer bread to oven and spray generously with water. Spray 2 more times at 3-minute intervals to steam. Bake baguettes until crust is brown, about 30 minutes. (Bake loaves 5 to 10 minutes longer.) Remove bread from oven and brush surface with ice water. Turn out onto wire racks and let cool before slicing.

Sourdough French Bread

1 loaf

Sponge
½ cup Basic Sourdough Starter (see following recipe), room temperature
1 cup lukewarm water (90°F to 105°F)
2 cups all purpose flour

1 teaspoon sugar
1 teaspoon salt
2 cups all purpose flour

2 to 3 tablespoons cornmeal

Boiling water
1 egg white, beaten

For sponge: Place starter in large bowl. Stir in water, blending well. Add 2 cups flour and mix thoroughly. Cover with plastic wrap and let stand in warm draft-free area overnight.

Grease another large bowl. Add sugar and salt to sponge and mix well. Gradually mix in remaining flour. Turn dough out onto very lightly floured surface and knead until smooth and elastic, about 5 to 10 minutes. Transfer dough to greased bowl, turning to coat all surfaces. Cover with plastic and let stand in warm draft-free area until doubled in volume, about 1 to 1½ hours.

Sprinkle baking sheet with cornmeal. Punch dough down and shape into loaf about 12 inches long. Transfer to baking sheet. Cover with plastic and let stand in warm draft-free area until doubled in volume, about 1 hour.

Position rack in center of oven and preheat to 400°F. Fill pie plate or cake pan with boiling water and set in bottom of oven. Make 3 slashes diagonally across top of loaf using tip of sharp knife. Brush loaf with some of egg white. Bake 10 minutes. Brush again with egg white. Continue baking until loaf is nicely browned, about 20 to 30 minutes. Remove from oven, transfer to wire rack and let cool before slicing.

Basic Sourdough Starter

Makes about 1½ cups

1 cup lukewarm purified water (90°F to 105°F)
⅓ cup instant nonfat dry milk
3 tablespoons lowfat plain yogurt

1 cup all purpose flour

Rinse 1½- to 2-quart glass or ceramic bowl with hot water several minutes and wipe dry. Combine water and dry milk in bowl, stirring until milk is dissolved. Blend in yogurt. Cover with plastic wrap and let stand in warm draft-free area until consistency of yogurt, about 12 to 24 hours.

Using plastic spoon, gradually add flour, blending until smooth. Cover and let stand in warm draft-free area until mixture is full of bubbles and has sour aroma, about 2 to 4 days. The starter is now ready to use. Store covered in refrigerator in plastic or ceramic container (do not use glass).

Sourdough Whole Wheat Bread

1 loaf

Sponge
1½ teaspoons dry yeast
¼ cup lukewarm water (90°F to 105°F)
6 tablespoons Basic Sourdough Starter (see preceding recipe), room temperature
3 tablespoons instant nonfat dry milk
¾ cup lukewarm water (90°F to 105°F)
1½ cups stone-ground wheat flour

½ cup all purpose flour
2 tablespoons wheat germ

2 tablespoons molasses
2 tablespoons polyunsaturated margarine
1½ teaspoons salt
½ teaspoon baking soda
1¼ to 1¾ cups all purpose flour

For sponge: Dissolve yeast in ¼ cup lukewarm water in large bowl and let stand 5 minutes to proof. Add starter, dry milk and remaining warm water and blend well. Add wheat flour, all purpose flour and wheat germ and beat 4 to 5 minutes. Cover with plastic and let stand in warm draft-free area until doubled in volume, about 1 hour.

Add molasses, margarine, salt, baking soda and 1¼ cups all purpose flour and beat until dough is stiff, adding remaining ½ cup all purpose flour as necessary. Turn dough out onto very lightly floured surface and knead 10 to 15 minutes. Transfer to bowl. Cover dough and let stand in warm draft-free area until doubled, about 1½ hours.

Grease 9 × 5-inch loaf pan. Punch dough down and shape into loaf. Transfer to pan. Cover and let stand in warm draft-free area about 45 minutes.

Preheat oven to 375°F. Bake until loaf is nicely browned, about 35 minutes.

Crusty Whole Wheat Bread

For a crisp crust, bake this country loaf in a heavy dark steel French bread pan placed on a preheated baking stone. A lighter-colored pan or baking sheet can be used, but the crust will be softer in texture.

1 loaf

1 tablespoon cornmeal

1 envelope dry yeast
1 teaspoon sugar
1 cup plus 2 tablespoons warm water (105°F to 115°F)

2¼ cups cake flour (9 ounces)

¾ cup whole wheat flour (4 ounces)
1½ teaspoons salt

¼ cup (about) all purpose flour

1 egg
½ teaspoon salt

Generously grease baking sheet or French bread pan and sprinkle with cornmeal. Oil large mixing bowl.

Combine yeast, sugar and water and let proof about 10 minutes.

Combine cake and wheat flours with salt in work bowl of processor fitted with Steel Knife. With machine running, pour yeast mixture through feed tube and process 20 to 30 seconds. *Dough should be moist, spongy and elastic.* Transfer dough to oiled bowl, turning to coat entire surface. Cover with very damp towel and set in oven that has been preheated to lowest temperature setting for 2 minutes and then turned off, cushioning the bottom of bowl with pot holder or folded towel. Allow dough to rise until doubled in bulk, about 1½ hours.

Sprinkle board heavily with remaining flour. Set dough on board and work in flour with your hands until dough is easy to handle and no longer sticky. Roll dough into rectangle ½ inch thick and 1 inch shorter on either side than baking sheet or French bread pan. Roll up into oblong loaf, pinching ends and seam tightly. Place seam side down on prepared baking sheet. Let rise until doubled in bulk, about 1½ hours.

If letting dough rise in oven, remove and set aside. Position rack in center of oven and arrange six 6 × 6-inch quarry tiles over rack. Preheat oven to 425°F. Beat egg with salt for glaze. When dough has doubled, slash top with Steel Knife. Brush surface of loaf with glaze, being careful not to drip glaze onto pan. Place pan directly on tiles and bake until loaf sounds hollow when tapped on bottom, about 25 to 30 minutes. Cool on wire rack before slicing.

If quarry tiles are unavailable, set a second baking sheet in oven while preheating. Place baking sheet or pan with dough on top of preheated baking sheet.

Quick Brown Bread

1 round loaf

1½ cups white bread flour or all purpose flour
1½ cups whole wheat flour
1 cup rye flour
2 teaspoons baking powder

1 teaspoon baking soda
½ teaspoon salt
¼ cup molasses or honey
1¼ to 1½ cups buttermilk, room temperature

Preheat oven to 375°F. Grease baking sheet. Combine flours, baking powder, baking soda and salt in large bowl of electric mixer. Beat on medium speed until evenly mixed, stopping to scrape down sides of bowl. Stir in molasses and enough buttermilk to make soft, pliable dough. Beat on high speed until mixture comes away from sides of bowl, about 3 minutes (to activate gluten).

Turn dough out onto lightly floured surface and knead until smooth, about 2 minutes. Pat into circle 2 inches thick. Transfer to prepared sheet. Using sharp knife or razor blade, cut a wide cross ½ inch deep in center of dough. Bake until loaf is brown and sounds hollow when tapped, about 55 minutes (bread will split open at cross). Cool on rack.

For variation, ½ cup wheat germ, bran flour or cornmeal or 2 tablespoons soy flour or barley flour may be substituted for an equal amount of rye or whole wheat flour.

Enriched Quick Bread: Mix flours, baking powder, baking soda and salt as above. Using pastry blender or 2 knives, cut in ¼ cup well-chilled butter (cut into 8 pieces). When mixture resembles coarse meal, stir in lightly beaten egg (room temperature) with half of liquid. Add remaining liquid as needed to make soft, pliable dough.

Quick Fruit or Nut Bread: After adding flour, stir in ½ cup chopped nuts and/or chopped dried fruit such as raisins, figs, apricots or dates that have been presoaked in boiling water for 30 minutes and then thoroughly drained.

Emerald Isle Bread

3 small loaves

1¼ cups rolled oats
3 cups all purpose flour
1½ tablespoons baking powder
2 teaspoons salt
2 cups milk

¼ cup honey
¼ cup minced fresh parsley
1 egg
1 tablespoon melted butter

Preheat oven to 350°F. Generously grease three 6 × 3 × 2¼-inch loaf pans. Grind oats in processor or blender until fine. Transfer to mixing bowl. Add flour, baking powder and salt and mix well. Whisk together milk, honey, parsley and egg. Add to dry ingredients, blending with wooden spoon until well combined. Divide batter evenly among pans. Bake until loaves test done, about 50 minutes. Turn out onto rack and brush tops with melted butter.

Pesto Pizza Bread

2 pizzas

Pesto Sauce
2 cups tightly packed fresh basil leaves (about 1 large bunch)
½ cup olive oil
⅓ cup pine nuts, toasted
1 large garlic clove
1 teaspoon salt
½ teaspoon freshly ground pepper
2 ounces freshly grated imported Parmesan cheese
1 ounce freshly grated Pecorino Romano cheese

Pizza Bread
Cornmeal
2⅔ cups warm water (105°F to 115°F)

1 envelope dry yeast
2 teaspoons sugar

⅓ cup olive oil
1 tablespoon salt
5½ cups (about) unbleached all purpose flour or bread flour

1 egg lightly beaten with 1 tablespoon water

For sauce: Combine first 6 ingredients in processor or blender and puree, stopping machine as necessary to scrape down sides of container. Pour into bowl. Stir in cheeses, cover and refrigerate. (Flavor is better if cheeses are grated and added just before using.)

For bread: Grease two 14-inch pizza pans or heavy baking sheets and sprinkle with cornmeal. Oil large mixing bowl and set aside. Pour ⅔ cup warm water into another large bowl. Add yeast and sugar and stir until dissolved. Let mixture stand until foamy, about 10 minutes.

Stir in remaining water with olive oil and salt. Mix in about 5 cups of flour, 1 cup at a time, beating well with wooden spoon after each addition, until dough comes away from sides of bowl. Sprinkle work surface with ½ cup remaining flour. Turn dough out onto surface and knead until dough is smooth, shiny and elastic, adding more flour as necessary, about 10 minutes.

Transfer dough to oiled bowl, turning to coat all surfaces. Cover with towel and let stand in warm draft-free area until doubled, about 1½ hours.

Punch dough down, turn out onto floured surface and knead briefly into ball. Return to bowl, cover with towel and let stand in warm draft-free area until doubled again, about 1½ hours.

Punch dough down. Turn out onto lightly floured surface. Divide dough in half. Roll or pat each half into 14-inch circle. Transfer to prepared pans.

Pinch up edges of dough to form shallow rim. Brush twice with egg mixture. Divide pesto sauce evenly between crusts. Let stand in warm draft-free area for approximately 30 minutes.

Preheat oven to 400°F. Bake until crusts are golden brown, about 20 to 30 minutes. Let stand 5 minutes before cutting into wedges.

Bread may be wrapped in foil and refrigerated for several hours after baking. To reheat, sprinkle with water, wrap in foil and warm in 400°F oven for about 10 minutes.

For variation, arrange slices of Fontina, Bel Paese, mozzarella or provolone cheese over pesto sauce before baking.

Whole Wheat Ballons

24 rolls

1½ envelopes dry yeast or 1 ounce compressed yeast
¼ teaspoon sugar
1½ cups warm water (105°F to 115°F)
1 cup warm milk (105°F to 115°F)
2 tablespoons (¼ stick) unsalted butter, melted

2 teaspoons salt
3½ cups whole wheat flour
2 cups (about) unbleached all purpose flour
½ cup bran

Dissolve yeast and sugar in warm water in large mixing bowl. Blend in milk, butter and salt. Stir in whole wheat flour. Add enough all purpose flour to make soft dough. Turn out onto floured surface and knead, adding flour as necessary, until dough no longer feels sticky and is firm and elastic, at least 10 minutes. Place in oiled bowl, turning to coat entire surface. Cover with towel and let stand in warm draft-free area until doubled, about 1½ hours.

Oil baking sheet. Turn dough out onto lightly floured surface and knead again, adding more flour if dough is sticky. Divide dough into 24 portions. On unfloured surface, roll each portion into ball using flat palm of hand, exerting a good deal of pressure directly down onto ball. Roll and press until dough tenses and tightens. Lightly press 1 side of ball into bran. Place on oiled baking sheet. Cover loosely with towel and let stand in warm draft-free area until doubled, about 30 minutes.

Preheat oven to 400°F. Just before baking, use single-edged razor blade to make light slit through only the very top surface of each ball across the center. Bake until golden, about 15 to 20 minutes. Cool on racks.

Hors d'Oeuvre Biscuits

48 biscuits

2 cups all purpose flour
2½ teaspoons baking powder
½ teaspoon salt
¼ cup (½ stick) butter, cut into small pieces

2 tablespoons chopped lard
⅔ cup (or more) half and half or milk

Melted butter

Preheat oven to 450°F. Grease large baking sheet. Sift flour, baking powder and salt into large bowl. Cut in butter and lard until mixture resembles coarse meal. Make well in center. Pour in ⅔ cup half and half, then gradually incorporate flour mixture using fork or flexible rubber spatula. Sprinkle additional drops of half and half over any unmoistened flour.

Turn dough out onto lightly floured surface. Knead 10 times. Roll out into rectangle ¼ inch thick. Cut out biscuits using 1½- or 2-inch floured fluted biscuit cutter. Arrange closely on prepared baking sheet. Gently gather scraps together and repeat rolling and cutting. Brush biscuits with melted butter. Bake until golden brown, about 12 minutes.

Rye-Caraway Pretzels

18 pretzels

1 package dry yeast or 1 cake compressed yeast
½ cup warm water (105°F to 115°F)
⅓ cup firmly packed brown sugar
1½ teaspoons salt
2 teaspoons caraway seed
2 cups milk, scalded
3 cups light rye flour

2½ cups unbleached all purpose flour
1 teaspoon baking powder

7 cups (about) water
2 tablespoons salt
1 egg white, lightly beaten
Coarse salt

Soften yeast in warm water and add sugar and salt. Soften caraway seed in scalded milk until milk is lukewarm, then combine with yeast mixture. Beat in 2 cups rye flour. Cover with damp cloth and let rise in warm area 1 hour. Preheat oven to between 375°F and 400°F. Generously grease baking sheet. Mix remaining rye and all purpose flours with baking powder and stir into sponge 1 cup at a time. Turn dough out onto lightly floured board and knead several minutes, adding more all purpose flour if dough is too sticky.

Stretch and pat dough into rectangle about 9 × 13 inches. Using sharp knife, cut dough into strips about ½ inch wide. With floured hands, roll strips into 18-inch strands and tie loosely into circular pretzel shape.

When all strips are tied, combine water and salt and bring to rapid boil. Using slotted spoon or spatula, carefully lower pretzels one at a time into water for 3 to 4 seconds. Remove and shake off excess water. Space pretzels about 1 inch apart on baking sheet. Brush with egg white and sprinkle with salt. Bake until nicely golden, about 18 to 20 minutes. Cool on racks.

Sesame Cheese Crisps

60 crisps

Glaze
  1 **large egg**
  ½ **teaspoon salt**

Crisps
  ¼ **pound (4 ounces) well-chilled sharp New York cheddar cheese, shredded**
  6 **tablespoons (¾ stick) butter, cut into thirds**

  3 **tablespoons water**
  2 **tablespoons sesame seed**
  1 **teaspoon dry mustard**
  1 **teaspoon hot pepper sauce**
  ½ **teaspoon salt**
  1 **cup unbleached flour**
  1 **teaspoon baking powder**

  Flour
  Sesame seed

Preheat oven to 350°F. Generously grease 2 baking sheets and sprinkle lightly with water. Set aside.

Combine egg and salt for glaze.

Mix cheese, butter, water, sesame seed, mustard, hot pepper sauce and salt and blend well. Add flour and baking powder and mix just until flour is blended in. Wrap dough in plastic and refrigerate at least 1 hour.

Divide dough in half. Roll 1 portion on floured board to ¼-inch thickness and cut out 1-inch rounds. Repeat with remaining dough. Transfer to prepared baking sheet and apply glaze carefully with feather brush or fingers. Sprinkle with sesame seed. Bake until lightly browned, about 15 minutes.

Homemade Taco Chips

4 to 6 servings

  12 **corn tortillas**
  2 **cups (about) vegetable oil**

  Salt

Cut tortillas into wedges. Heat oil in skillet to about 390°F. Fry tortilla wedges in batches until crisp. Drain on paper towels. Salt lightly and serve.

5 🍎 Hot Appetizers

Any visitor to France who is confronted by a good selection of *hors d'oeuvres chauds* on a restaurant menu has something of a dilemma. How to choose? Well (the waiter will probably say), it is not necessary to have only one; take a plate with several. *Bon.* Out comes the *plate dégustation,* and its collection of hot morsels is quickly devoured. So—why not another plate, with different hot appetizers? And so it goes, sometimes until the list is exhausted and all thoughts of a fish course or an entrée are put aside for another meal.

The same thing is likely to happen with Italian *antipasti caldi,* the Chinese steamed or fried dumplings called *dim sum,* Spanish *tapas* or any number of other international specialties. Hot appetizers are temptingly varied, from crisp fritters of vegetables or seafood to skewered kebabs of poultry or meat, baked stuffed clams, peppers or mushrooms to steamed pork dumplings, bountifully filled crepes to meatballs in a tangy sauce. And they are so substantial you may find yourself wanting not only to begin the meal with them, but also end it there as well. It is no wonder, then, that the buffet of hot appetizers has become one of the most popular ways to feed large gatherings.

And its popularity is all the greater for the fact that most hot appetizers are as convenient to make and serve as their cold counterparts. Many deep-fried morsels, such as Asparagus Cheese Fritters (page 82) or the Shrimp Egg Rolls on page 90, can be refrigerated or frozen and just popped into the oven to be reheated before serving. More delicate fritters that must be served fresh, such as Fried Zucchini Flowers (page 85) or Fritto Misto (page 91), are still easy to fry in several batches and keep warm briefly in the oven (see box, page 86). Other hot appetizers are assembled and done so quickly that there is no need even to consider cooking them in advance: skewers of Indonesian saté (pages 97, 101 and 102) or chunks of Spanish sausage in wine (page 107) are cooked in less than 15 minutes.

Like the selection of hot hors d'oeuvres on a fine French menu, the keynote of a successful hot appetizer buffet will be variety, encompassing a wide range of ingredients, textures and flavors. And while the restaurant diner may at first consider such a wide choice a dilemma, your guests at a hot appetizer buffet will approach it only with delight.

Vegetables and Cheese

Asparagus Cheese Fritters

The crisp cheese-flavored batter is a pleasing counterpoint to the crunchy-firm asparagus tip inside.

24 appetizers

24 fresh asparagus spears
Boiling water

1½ cups all purpose flour
½ teaspoon baking powder
Salt and freshly ground pepper
¾ cup finely grated Gruyère cheese
½ teaspoon grated lemon peel

1¼ cups milk
1 egg
Dash of Worcestershire sauce

Oil for deep frying
Lemon wedges and parsley sprigs
(garnish)

Wash, trim and cut asparagus about ½ inch below tips; reserve tender part of stems for soups or stews. Blanch tips in large amount of boiling water 1 minute. Drain immediately and dry well with paper towels.

Sift together flour, baking powder, salt and pepper in mixing bowl. Add grated cheese and lemon peel and blend well. In separate measuring cup or bowl, beat together milk, egg and Worcestershire. Slowly stir into dry mixture and blend completely (mixture should be fairly thick, almost the consistency of sour cream). Let stand 30 minutes at room temperature, or cover and refrigerate up to 2 hours. If mixture becomes too thick, thin with small amount of milk.

To cook, heat 2 to 3 inches oil to 375°F in deep fryer or large skillet. Using long-handled fork or spoon, individually dip asparagus tips into batter and deep fry several seconds on each side until puffed and golden. Remove with slotted spoon and drain well on paper towels. Transfer to heated serving platter and keep warm. When cooking is completed, decorate platter with lemon wedges and parsley sprigs and serve immediately.

Fritters can be frozen. To reheat, arrange on baking sheet and bake in 400°F oven 10 to 12 minutes.

Grilled Mushrooms with Marrow and Herbs

12 servings

¼ cup olive oil
¼ cup fresh lemon juice
1 1-inch piece green onion (white part only), quartered
1 garlic clove, halved
1 parsley sprig
1 teaspoon fresh thyme, snipped or ⅓ teaspoon dried, crumbled
½ teaspoon fresh rosemary, snipped or ⅛ teaspoon dried, crumbled

½ teaspoon salt
⅛ teaspoon freshly ground pepper
36 medium mushroom caps
3 ounces beef marrow, cut into 36 ¼-inch pieces

Parsley sprigs (garnish)

Combine first 9 ingredients in processor or blender and mix until herbs are finely minced. Brush each mushroom generously with herb mixture and arrange stem side up on rack placed over baking sheet. Top each mushroom with a piece of marrow. Cover and let stand at room temperature 1 day or refrigerate overnight. (Bring to room temperature before cooking.)

Just before serving, position broiler pan about 4 inches from heat source and preheat. Arrange mushrooms on pan and broil until marrow is almost melted, about 4 minutes. Transfer mushrooms to platter and garnish with parsley.

Baked Mushrooms

4 servings

12 medium mushrooms, wiped clean, stems removed and chopped
Olive oil
½ cup seasoned breadcrumbs

¼ cup chopped black olives
6 tablespoons marinara sauce (homemade or commercial)
3 tablespoons freshly grated Parmesan cheese

Preheat oven to 350°F. Roll each mushroom cap in small amount of olive oil and place on baking sheet or dish. Combine remaining ingredients including stems and divide evenly among mushrooms. Bake 10 minutes, just to heat through.

Sweet and Sour Glazed Onions

4 servings

1 quart (4 cups) water
1 pound small white onions, about 1 inch in diameter, unpeeled

⅓ to ½ cup Sherry vinegar

3 tablespoons olive oil
2 tablespoons sugar
Salt and freshly ground pepper

Bring water to boil in large saucepan. Add onions and boil 1 minute. Remove from heat, drain in colander and rinse with cold water. Trim off stem and root ends, then slip off skins.

Combine vinegar, oil, sugar, salt and pepper in large nonaluminum skillet. Add onions, cover and cook over medium-low heat about 25 minutes, or until onions are tender. If much liquid remains in skillet, remove lid, increase heat and boil until syrupy. Remove from heat, transfer to bowl and cool. Cover and refrigerate 1 or 2 days to mellow flavors. Reheat before serving. Spear with toothpicks and serve hot from chafing dish.

Spinach Balls

70 appetizers

2 10-ounce packages frozen chopped spinach, thawed and squeezed dry
2 cups herb stuffing mix, crushed
1 cup firmly packed freshly grated Parmesan cheese (5-ounce wedge)
½ cup (1 stick) butter, melted

4 small green onions, finely chopped
3 eggs
Dash of freshly grated nutmeg

Mustard Sauce (see following recipe)

Combine all ingredients except sauce in large bowl and mix well. Shape into 1-inch balls. Cover and refrigerate or freeze until ready to bake.

Preheat oven to 350°F. Set balls on ungreased baking sheet and bake until golden brown, about 10 to 15 minutes. Serve with Mustard Sauce.

Mustard Sauce

Makes about 1¼ cups

½ cup dry mustard
½ cup white vinegar

¼ cup sugar
1 egg yolk

Combine mustard and vinegar in small bowl. Cover and let stand at room temperature 4 hours.

Mix sugar and egg yolk in small saucepan. Add mustard-vinegar mixture and cook over low heat, stirring constantly, until slightly thickened. Cover and chill. Serve at room temperature.

Spinach Timbales with Fonduta

12 servings

1 pound Italian Fontina cheese, cubed
1 cup milk or half and half

Spinach Timbales
   Breadcrumbs
6 large bunches fresh spinach, stemmed
2 tablespoons butter

1 tablespoon butter
1 large shallot or 1 small onion, minced
1 cup whipping cream

1½ ounces Italian Fontina cheese, diced

6 eggs
3 egg yolks
2 tablespoons fresh lemon juice
¾ teaspoon salt
¼ teaspoon freshly ground pepper
¼ teaspoon freshly grated nutmeg

4 egg yolks
3 tablespoons butter
¼ teaspoon freshly ground white pepper

Combine Fontina with milk in medium bowl. Cover and refrigerate overnight.

For timbales: Preheat oven to 325°F. Generously butter two 6-cup muffin pans and sprinkle with breadcrumbs. Wash spinach thoroughly and shake off excess water. Melt 2 tablespoons butter in large heavy skillet over medium-high heat. Gradually add spinach, turning frequently, then cover and cook, stirring occasionally, until spinach is completely wilted, about 5 minutes. Transfer to colander and drain well; let cool. Squeeze dry by twisting in towel. Chop spinach finely and set aside.

Melt 1 tablespoon butter in same skillet. Add shallot, cover and cook over low heat, stirring occasionally, until translucent, about 7 minutes. Return spinach to skillet. Stir in cream a little at a time until absorbed. Transfer mixture to large bowl, stir in 1½ ounces diced Fontina cheese and cool.

Mix in eggs, 3 egg yolks, lemon juice, salt, pepper and nutmeg. Spoon mixture evenly into prepared muffin pan. Cover pan with buttered waxed paper. Set in larger pan. Add enough hot water to larger pan to come about ¾ up side of muffin pan. Bake until timbales are puffed and tester inserted in center comes out clean, about 25 minutes. Remove timbales from oven and keep warm in water bath.

Whisk remaining egg yolks in medium saucepan over low heat (or in top of double boiler set over simmering water), beating constantly until thickened. Add Fontina-milk mixture and whisk until well blended. Blend in butter 1 tablespoon at a time. Season fonduta with pepper. Remove from heat.

Just before serving, run sharp thin knife around each timbale, invert onto serving platter and spoon fonduta over.

Timbales can be prepared 2 days ahead, covered and refrigerated. Bring to room temperature before baking.

Spinach Palacsinta

4 to 6 servings

1 cup all purpose flour
⅛ teaspoon salt
6 eggs, separated
1 cup milk
½ cup whipping cream
6 tablespoons (¾ stick) melted unsalted butter or margarine
1 10-ounce package frozen chopped spinach, thawed and squeezed dry

½ cup vegetable oil

   Sour cream
½ cup freshly grated Parmesan cheese
⅛ teaspoon sweet Hungarian paprika

Combine flour and salt in mixing bowl and blend well. Add yolks one at a time, beating mixture into thick paste. Gradually add milk, then cream, beating constantly until mixture is smooth. Stir in butter, then spinach, mixing well.

Beat egg whites in separate bowl until stiff. Stir ¼ of whites into spinach mixture to loosen. Fold in remaining whites gently but thoroughly.

Brush 8-inch skillet with some of oil and place over medium heat. Place 2 tablespoons batter in center of pan, tilting to spread to diameter of about 3 to 4 inches (do not try to cover bottom of pan with batter).

Cook until edges are slightly browned. Turn and cook second side until lightly browned. Transfer to plate and cover with waxed paper. Repeat with remaining batter, coating pan with oil before cooking each pancake and stirring through batter before adding to pan.

Preheat oven to 375°F. Butter baking sheet. Arrange palacsintas in stacks of 3 on baking sheet, spreading thin layer of sour cream between each and sprinkling layers with Parmesan cheese. Bake until heated through, about 10 to 15 minutes. Place stacks on serving plates and sprinkle with additional Parmesan. Top with sour cream and sprinkle with paprika. Serve immediately.

Eggplant with Prosciutto and Bel Paese

12 servings

2 pounds eggplant, peeled, cut crosswise into twelve ¾-inch slices
¼ cup (½ stick) butter, melted
   Freshly ground pepper
4 ounces thinly sliced prosciutto

1¼ pounds Italian Bel Paese or Italian Fontina cheese, cut into thin slices

Chicory or escarole leaves (garnish)

Preheat oven to 375°F. Grease baking sheet. Arrange eggplant slices on sheet and brush with butter. Sprinkle lightly with pepper. Completely cover each slice with single layer of prosciutto. Top with cheese, pressing lightly.

Bake until eggplant is tender, easily pierced with knife and cheese is melted and brown, about 10 to 15 minutes. Arrange on serving platter and garnish with chicory or escarole.

Fried Zucchini Flowers

Zucchini have both male and female flowers. The actual vegetable is the stem of the female flower, and the flowers are not as good for eating. The male, on the other hand, produces a bright orange blossom and develops only a small thin stem that does not grow into a vegetable. If you have no access to a garden, use more readily available spinach leaves.

16 appetizers

Batter
¾ cup plus 2 tablespoons all purpose flour
¼ teaspoon salt
1½ tablespoons olive oil
1 egg yolk
   Pinch of freshly grated nutmeg
3 tablespoons dry white wine

¾ cup cold water

   Oil for deep frying
1 egg white
16 male zucchini flowers or 16 small spinach leaves
   Salt

For batter: Sift flour and salt into medium bowl. Add next 5 ingredients one at a time in order given, blending well and making sure batter is smooth. Cover and let stand at cool room temperature (do not refrigerate) for 2 hours.

When ready to serve, heat oil for deep frying to 375°F. Beat egg white until stiff. Fold into batter, blending well. Dip flowers one at a time into batter and add to oil (do not crowd). Fry until golden brown, about 1 minute per side. Remove with strainer or slotted spoon and drain on paper towels. Transfer to dish, sprinkle with salt and serve.

🍎 *Deep Frying Guidelines*

If you don't have an electric fry pan with built-in thermostat, use a heavy large stockpot, Dutch oven or casserole that won't tip easily (long-handled pots should be avoided). A wok is ideal since it provides the largest frying area while using the smallest amount of oil. Several inches of oil are required so the food can float, but if it comes more than halfway up the sides of the pan, there is a risk of boiling over. Keep a lid and a supply of baking soda handy in case of excessive sputtering or a fire.

Paradoxically, deep-fried morsels should crust immediately upon coming into contact with the hot oil, absorbing less grease than pan-fried foods. But this quick seal can only come about if the fat is hot enough. Otherwise the food absorbs the fat, becoming greasy and soggy. Deep frying temperatures range between 375°F and 395°F. Use the lower heat for everything except precooked foods, small fish and batter- or crumb-covered items that disintegrate if they do not crust immediately. In the absence of a thermometer, test the temperature of the oil with a bread cube—the fat should bubble around it at 375°F; it will brown instantly at 395°F. Another test: The fat is ready to use if your hand feels intense heat when held three inches above it.

When the oil is hot, add batter- and crumb-coated foods one at a time without piercing coating—large tongs or a long-handled wire skimmer is good for this. Place other items in a fryer basket that has been preheated in the oil to prevent sticking. Immerse ingredients gradually to permit moisture to evaporate. Stir several times so food cooks on all sides and doesn't stick together.

Avoid overcrowding the fryer. If you have a small pot or a limited amount of oil, fry in batches, allowing the oil to return to the proper temperature before starting each batch. Cold food will also cause the temperature to fall.

Drain fried food in a single layer on a large baking sheet lined with crumpled paper towels. If cooking several batches, keep cooked food warm in a 200°F oven with door left ajar. To prevent sogginess, do not season food with salt or sugar until just before eating. Fried foods should be served as quickly as possible.

Zucchini Sticks

6 to 8 servings

Oil for deep frying
4 eggs
¼ cup whipping cream
½ teaspoon freshly ground pepper

¼ teaspoon salt
3 to 4 medium zucchini, quartered and cut into 2-inch lengths
¾ cup well-seasoned breadcrumbs

Preheat oil to 350°F. Mix next 4 ingredients in blender. Transfer to bowl. Dip zucchini into egg mixture, then coat with breadcrumbs. Add to oil in batches and fry until browned and crisp, 3 to 4 minutes. Drain on paper towels. Serve hot.

Zucchini Cups with Fennel

8 servings

4 medium zucchini at least 1½ inches in diameter (2 pounds total), unpeeled, trimmed
1½ teaspoons salt

¼ cup (½ stick) unsalted butter
1 large fennel bulb (¾ pound), greens trimmed and discarded, coarsely chopped*

1 small onion (2 ounces), minced
1 small garlic clove, minced
½ teaspoon dried thyme
  Salt and freshly ground pepper
½ cup parsley leaves, minced

Cut zucchini into cylinders 1½ to 2 inches long. Using small melon baller, scoop out center leaving ½ inch at base and ¼ inch on sides. Coarsely chop pulp. Sprinkle shells with salt, invert on paper towels and drain 30 minutes.

Position rack in center of oven and preheat to 350°F. Melt butter in sauté pan or small skillet. Add zucchini pulp, fennel, onion, garlic, thyme, salt and pepper and sauté over medium heat until vegetables are heated through but still crisp, about 10 minutes. Drain liquid into small pan and reduce to a glaze over medium-high heat. Return to sauté pan and stir in parsley. Season to taste.

Pat zucchini dry with paper towels. Fill with fennel mixture. Place in flat ovenproof dish and add ¼ inch water. Cover with foil and bake 30 minutes. Remove foil and bake another 10 to 20 minutes. (*Do not overcook; zucchini should be slightly al dente.*)

*If fennel is unavailable, substitute ¾ pound celery and 1 teaspoon fennel seed.

Roasted Stuffed Peppers with Anchovies

12 servings

4 red bell peppers
4 green bell peppers
4 yellow bell peppers*

Stuffing
2 tablespoons olive oil
1 large shallot, minced
3 ounces pancetta, minced
7 anchovy fillets, minced
2 ounces pistachio nuts, shelled and coarsely chopped
1½ cups breadcrumbs
1 large garlic clove, minced
⅓ cup whipping cream

1 egg, lightly beaten

1 ounce freshly grated Pecorino Romano cheese
¼ teaspoon dried oregano, crumbled
¼ teaspoon dried marjoram, crumbled
1 tablespoon minced fresh parsley (preferably Italian flat leaf)
¼ teaspoon freshly ground pepper
  Salt
  Olive oil

24 rolled anchovy fillets with capers (garnish)

Preheat broiler. Broil peppers 4 inches from heat source until each side is just charred. Transfer to plastic bag. Wrap tightly and let stand 5 minutes. Peel peppers and cut in half, discarding stems and seeds. Rinse peppers; pat dry with paper towels and set aside.

Heat olive oil in medium saucepan over low heat. Add shallot, cover and cook until translucent, about 7 minutes. Add pancetta, anchovies and pistachios and continue cooking, stirring until anchovies have dissolved, about 1 minute.

Add breadcrumbs and garlic, increase heat slightly and stir until breadcrumbs are lightly browned, about 3 minutes. Stir in cream 1 tablespoon at a time until absorbed. Transfer stuffing to bowl and let cool.

Add next 7 ingredients to stuffing and mix well. Brush gratin or other shallow baking dish with olive oil. Spread generous spoonful of stuffing into each pepper half. Roll peppers up; transfer to pan seam side down. Brush each pepper generously with additional olive oil. Cover and let stand at room temperature 1 day or chill up to 2 days (bring to room temperature before baking).

Preheat oven to 375°F. Bake peppers until heated through, about 30 minutes. Top each with rolled anchovy. Serve hot or at room temperature.

*Substitute additional red and/or green peppers if yellow are unavailable.

Deep-Fried Cheese

6 appetizers

2 eggs
½ cup (8 tablespoons) fine dry breadcrumbs

Oil for deep frying
¼ pound Swiss or Gruyère cheese, cut into 1-inch cubes

Beat eggs with 2 tablespoons breadcrumbs in small bowl. Place remaining breadcrumbs in another small bowl. Pour oil into small skillet to depth of 2 inches and heat to 380°F. Dip cheese into egg mixture and then into breadcrumbs, coating well. Fry in batches until crisp and golden, about 1 minute. Remove with slotted spoon or small strainer, transfer to paper towels and drain well. Spear cubes with toothpicks and serve immediately.

Foglie de Salvia Ripiene

15 appetizers

1 cup sifted all purpose flour
3 tablespoons dry white wine
2 tablespoons olive oil
1 egg, separated
  Pinch of salt
¾ cup (about) cold water

½ pound mozzarella cheese, cut into 1-inch squares ¼ inch thick

30 small sage leaves (preferably Italian)

Oil for deep frying
Salt

Combine flour, wine, oil, egg yolk and salt in medium bowl with enough cold water to make batter consistency of whipping cream. Cover and let stand at cool room temperature (do not refrigerate) for about 2 hours.

Layer 3 squares of cheese with 2 sage leaves to form each appetizer. Secure with plain wooden toothpicks.

When ready to serve, heat oil for deep frying to 375°F. Beat egg white until stiff. Fold into batter, blending well. Dip each cube in batter and add to oil in batches. Fry until golden brown on all sides. Drain well on paper towels. Arrange on platter, sprinkle lightly with salt and serve immediately.

Ham and Fennel Seed
Terrine, Shrimp Mousse
with Avocado Surprise

Pancakes with Seven Fillings and Sauce

Clockwise from top: Quick Glassblower's Herring, Mini-Swedish Meatballs, Bird's Nest, Beet Salad, Marinated Shrimp and Cucumber, Dilled Mushrooms

Galantine de Canard à l'Orange

Top to bottom: Ceviche, Shrimp in Green Cheese Sauce, Carnitas, Cold Mexican Rice, Refritos

Clockwise from top left: Filled Tartlets and Barquettes, Mini-Crepes with Asparagus, Artichoke Bottoms with Paté, Snail-stuffed Mushrooms, Marinated Vegetable Medley, Curried Chicken Pufflets

*Clockwise from top: Butterflied Leg of Lamb; Jerusalem
Artichoke Salad; Sole, Salmon and Scallop Mousse with
Sauce Verte; Mushrooms Pactole; Chicken Circassian
with Walnut Sauce; Cauliflower, Carrot and Squash Salad*

Queso

This delicious appetizer is based on a recipe from Armando's, one of Houston's most popular Mexican restaurants.

18 to 20 servings

1 pound Monterey Jack, mozzarella or Havarti cheese, grated

3 tablespoons vegetable oil
1 large yellow onion, chopped

½ cup chopped green bell pepper
1 pound mushrooms, sliced

½ cup whipping cream
18 to 20 flour tortillas, warmed

Preheat oven to 200°F. Spread cheese evenly in shallow glass baking dish or casserole and place in oven until partially melted, about 10 minutes.

Meanwhile, heat oil in large skillet over medium-high heat. Add onion and pepper and sauté 3 to 4 minutes. Add mushrooms and cook, stirring frequently, until mushrooms are moist and slightly darkened, 4 to 5 minutes.

Remove cheese from oven and gradually blend in cream, stirring until well mixed. Add mushroom mixture and any liquid in pan a little at a time, blending thoroughly. Bring immediately to table and spoon over tortillas.

 *Seafood*

Shrimp in Red Rioja Wine

6 servings

1 onion, finely minced
1 large garlic clove, finely minced
2 tablespoons olive oil
1 cup dry red Rioja wine

1 pound cooked shrimp, with or without shells
Salt and freshly ground pepper

Sauté onion and garlic in olive oil until just transparent. Add wine and simmer until sauce is slightly reduced. Add shrimp and heat through. Season to taste with salt and pepper. Serve hot or cold.

Shrimp with Curry Dipping Sauce

4 to 6 servings

1 pound uncooked shrimp, shelled and deveined (tails intact)
2 bay leaves

Curry Dipping Sauce
2 tablespoons (¼ stick) unsalted butter
½ cup finely chopped yellow onion

½ cup peeled chopped apples
1 medium banana, chopped
3 tablespoons mango chutney
2 teaspoons curry powder
Ground red pepper
1 cup chicken stock
Herb or vegetable salt

Cook shrimp with bay leaves in boiling water until just pink. Drain well. Discard bay leaves. Refrigerate.

For sauce: Melt butter in large skillet over medium heat. Add onion, apples, banana, chutney and curry powder. Season with ground red pepper to taste. Cook 3 minutes, stirring constantly. Add stock and bring to boil. Reduce heat and simmer 2 minutes. Season with herb salt to taste. Transfer mixture to blender or processor (in batches if necessary) and puree. Return sauce to skillet, place over medium heat and simmer 5 minutes.

Sauce can be refrigerated 1 to 2 days.

Indonesian Shrimp Saté

10 servings

2 tablespoons vegetable oil
2 garlic cloves, minced
¼ cup fresh lemon juice
3 tablespoons peanut butter
1 tablespoon finely minced green onion

2 teaspoons light soy sauce
1 teaspoon chili powder
1 teaspoon turmeric

3 dozen medium or large shrimp, shelled and deveined

Heat oil in small skillet over low heat. Add garlic and cook until lightly browned. Stir in all remaining ingredients except shrimp (mixture will be very thick) and simmer, stirring constantly, for 1 minute. Let cool.

Add shrimp and mix with fingers until well coated. Let stand 30 minutes at room temperature, or cover tightly and refrigerate overnight.

Prepare hibachi or barbecue, or preheat broiler. Thread 3 shrimp through tail and head onto each skewer. Cook about 3 to 4 inches from heat source until crisp and brown, about 3 minutes on each side; *do not overcook.*

Shrimp Egg Rolls

48 appetizers

14 ounces Chinese celery cabbage (Napa), sliced horizontally

Shrimp Filling
1½ cups cooked shrimp, coarsely chopped
8 water chestnuts, minced
6 large green onions (4 ounces total), thinly sliced

2 tablespoons peanut butter
1 tablespoon sesame oil
1 tablespoon light soy sauce
Salt

10 egg roll skins
1 egg

Oil for deep frying

The day before assembling egg rolls, cook cabbage in boiling salted water for 30 seconds. Transfer to colander and run under cold water until cabbage is cold to the touch. Drain. Wrap in towels to absorb as much moisture as possible, changing towels as they become saturated. Refrigerate cabbage in towels overnight. (Cooked, "dried" celery cabbage should measure ⅔ to ¾ cup.)

Combine cabbage with all ingredients for filling and mix thoroughly using your hands. Taste and adjust seasoning; filling should be highly seasoned.

Forming and cooking: It is important to roll each cylinder tightly if you plan to serve egg rolls sliced. For each egg roll, shape about 3 tablespoons of filling with your hands into a firm cylinder about 4 inches long and 1 inch in diameter. Place cylinder diagonally across lower middle of egg roll skin. Roll lower flap tightly over filling, leaving upper triangle of wrapper exposed. Bring 2 side flaps securely across cylinder, making sure there are no unnecessary wrinkles or there is no looseness in the wrapper or oil will be retained in cooking. Lightly beat egg and use to brush exposed triangle. Roll wrapper into tight, neat package. Repeat with remaining filling and egg roll skins.

Pour oil into wok or deep fryer to depth of 3 inches and heat to 375°F or until a piece of green onion sizzles when dropped into the oil. Deep fry egg rolls 3 at a time until golden brown, about 2 minutes. Remove with slotted spoon and drain thoroughly on paper towels. *(Egg rolls can be wrapped in clean paper towels and refrigerated at this point. Reheat in 450°F oven 10 minutes; do not preheat oven.)* Slice with serrated knife and serve.

For extra-crisp egg rolls, deep fry a second time in hot (375°F) oil until dark brown. Drain thoroughly on paper towels, slice if desired and serve immediately.

Clam and Beer Appetizers

36 appetizers

½ cup (1 stick) butter, melted
½ cup breadcrumbs
¼ cup beer
1 small onion, minced
4 garlic cloves, minced
2 tablespoons minced fresh parsley
1½ teaspoons Italian seasoning

½ teaspoon oregano
Salt and freshly ground pepper
4 6½-ounce cans minced clams, drained (juice reserved)
36 toast rounds or clam shells

Preheat oven to 375°F. Lightly grease baking sheet. Combine first 8 ingredients with salt and pepper to taste and mix well. Add clams and blend thoroughly. If mixture seems too dry, moisten with reserved clam juice. Spread on toast rounds or spoon into shells. Bake 10 minutes. Remove from oven and heat broiler. Broil until tops are golden brown. Serve immediately.

Clams Marinara

6 to 12 servings

72 small clams in shells

1 minced large onion
5 tablespoons olive oil
2 large tomatoes, peeled and chopped

½ cup dry white Rioja wine
1 cup chopped parsley
Salt and freshly ground pepper
Crusty French bread

Soak clams in cold water for about 1 hour, then scrub thoroughly.

In a large Dutch oven, slowly sauté onion in olive oil until golden. Add tomatoes, stirring until slightly thickened. Add clams and wine. Cover and cook until clams have opened, about 5 to 10 minutes. Stir in parsley. Season to taste with salt and pepper. Serve with crusty bread.

Fritto Misto

Pat seafood and vegetables dry with paper towels before coating with batter.

6 servings

Batter
½ cup instant flour
¼ cup water
1 egg, separated
1 tablespoon dry vermouth
Salt and freshly ground pepper

6 large shrimp, peeled and deveined
¼ pound firm-fleshed fish fillets, cut into chunks

1 medium zucchini, cut into ½-inch chunks or 6 medium mushrooms or 6 frozen artichoke hearts, thawed or 1 Japanese eggplant, trimmed and cut into ½-inch slices or combination

Oil for deep frying
Lemon wedges (garnish)

For batter: Combine flour, water, egg yolk, vermouth, salt and pepper in medium bowl and stir until smooth. Beat egg white in separate bowl until stiff peaks form; fold into batter.

Dip seafood and vegetables into batter, coating well. Let stand 10 minutes.

Meanwhile, heat oil for deep frying to 370°F; preheat oven to lowest setting. Fry ingredients in batches until golden brown. Remove with slotted spoon and drain well on paper towels; keep warm in oven while frying balance of ingredients. Sprinkle seafood and vegetables with salt and pepper, garnish with lemon wedges and serve immediately.

Crabby Mushrooms

24 appetizers

1 6- to 6½-ounce can crabmeat or ½ pound fresh or thawed frozen crabmeat, rinsed and drained
2 teaspoons fresh lemon juice
⅓ cup finely chopped black olives
¼ cup mayonnaise
2 tablespoons chopped fresh parsley

¼ teaspoon garlic powder
¼ teaspoon onion powder
24 medium mushrooms, stems removed
Freshly grated Parmesan cheese

Preheat oven to 400°F. Toss crabmeat with lemon juice in medium bowl. Add next 5 ingredients and mix well. Fill mushroom caps with mixture. Sprinkle with cheese. Rinse baking sheet lightly with water, shaking off excess. Arrange mushrooms on sheet. Cover with foil and bake 12 to 15 minutes. Remove foil and continue baking until tops are golden, about 5 minutes. Serve immediately.

Oysters Midas

We've added watercress to Chef Gérard Drouillard's Belons au Champagne, one of the recipes that have made La Marée of Paris one of the city's most distinguished restaurants. Excellent with a chilled brut Champagne.

24 appetizers

24 fresh oysters on the half shell
⅔ cup oyster liquid or clam broth
½ cup Champagne or dry white wine
2 large shallots, minced (2 tablespoons)
Pinch of ground red pepper
½ cup crème fraîche

Hollandaise Sauce
3 egg yolks
1 tablespoon fresh lemon juice

¾ teaspoon salt
½ teaspoon freshly ground white pepper
1 cup (2 sticks) unsalted butter, sizzling hot

1 bunch watercress, stems trimmed

Combine oysters, their liquid or clam broth, Champagne or dry white wine in saucepan over medium heat and cook only until oysters are plumped; *do not boil.* Remove oysters with slotted spoon and set aside. Add shallot and ground red pepper to saucepan and boil until liquid is reduced to ½ cup. Strain out shallot. Stir in crème fraîche and cook vigorously until mixture measures ½ cup. Set aside this reduction and keep hot for flavoring hollandaise sauce.

For hollandaise sauce: Combine egg yolks, lemon juice, salt and pepper in food processor or blender. With machine running, drizzle hot butter into yolks. (Hollandaise will thicken as butter is slowly added. Reheat butter if it cools.) With machine running, slowly add hot reduction and mix well. Taste and adjust seasoning (oysters tend to require a generous amount).

Preheat broiler. Place a few watercress leaves in each oyster shell. Spoon 1 teaspoon of sauce into bottom. Top with oyster and spoon additional sauce over oysters. Broil 6 inches from heat source until sauce is browned, about 3 to 4 minutes, watching carefully to avoid burning. Serve immediately.

Oysters Aptos

12 appetizers

Rock salt
12 oysters on the half shell
3 strips bacon, partially cooked and cut into squares

2 tablespoons (¼ stick) butter
1 green onion (including 4 inches of green part), minced

¼ cup fresh French breadcrumbs
1 tablespoon fresh lemon juice
Salt and freshly ground pepper
Minced parsley (garnish)

Line bottom of shallow ovenproof baking dish with rock salt. Arrange oysters over salt. Top each with bacon.

Preheat oven to 400°F. Melt butter in small skillet over medium heat. Add onion and sauté until softened. Add breadcrumbs, lemon juice, salt and pepper and continue cooking until breadcrumbs begin to crisp. Spoon mixture evenly over oysters. Bake 6 minutes. Garnish with parsley and serve.

Clams may be substituted for oysters.

 Poultry

Spicy Chicken Wings

24 appetizers

24 disjointed chicken wings (tips discarded)
Garlic salt
Onion salt

Freshly ground pepper
Peanut Sauce (see following recipe)

Preheat broiler. Sprinkle chicken with garlic and onion salts and pepper. Place on rack and broil 4 to 6 inches from heat source until crisp and brown, about 3 to 5 minutes per side. Serve hot or at room temperature with sauce.

Peanut Sauce

Makes about 1 cup

¼ cup peach preserves
¼ cup whipping cream
¼ to ⅓ cup peanut butter

2 tablespoons soy sauce
1 tablespoon fresh lemon juice

Combine all ingredients in processor or blender. Serve at room temperature.

Cantonese Stuffed Chicken Wings

20 appetizers

20 chicken wings
1 whole large bamboo shoot

Marinade
½ cup dark soy sauce
3 tablespoons honey
2 tablespoons dry Sherry

1 tablespoon finely minced green onion
Freshly ground white pepper to taste

Chopped chives and green onion (garnish)

To bone wings: Remove small wing tips. Cut cartilage linking 2 bones in larger portion of wing (there is 1 large and 1 small bone). Push the 2 bones out. (Save smaller wing portion—the drumette—and use for another meal.)

Slice bamboo shoot into sticks the size of biggest wing bone. Stuff wing by inserting shoot into big bone cavity.

For marinade: Combine all ingredients in shallow pan. Add wings and marinate 1 hour, turning several times.

Preheat hibachi or barbecue, or preheat oven to 400°F. Grill wings over medium heat or on rack in shallow pan until crisp and brown, basting and turning as necessary. Transfer to platter. Garnish with chives and green onion and serve.

Paprikás Chicken-Filled Palacsinta

10 to 14 palacsintas

¼ cup (½ stick) unsalted butter
2 large onions, diced
5 tablespoons sweet Hungarian paprika
1 large garlic clove, minced
2 whole chicken breasts, halved, boned and skinned
1 medium-size green bell pepper, chopped

1 cup chicken broth

Salt and freshly ground white pepper

10 to 14 Basic Palacsinta Shells (see following recipe)

½ cup sour cream

Melt butter in large skillet over medium heat. Add onion and sauté until lightly colored. Add paprika and garlic and sauté briefly until garlic is softened. Add chicken and green pepper and sauté about 5 minutes. Add broth and simmer uncovered until chicken is tender. Remove chicken from skillet to cool; let onion mixture cool slightly.

Preheat oven to 350°F. Lightly grease 9 × 13-inch baking dish. Cut chicken into ½-inch cubes and place in large bowl. Puree onion mixture in processor or blender until smooth. Add half to chicken and toss until well coated; season with salt and white pepper.

Divide chicken among palacsinta shells. Fold up 1 edge, then fold in sides and roll envelope fashion. Place seam side down in single layer in prepared dish. Tent with foil and bake until heated through, about 20 minutes.

Bring remaining puree to boiling point in small saucepan. Remove from heat and stir 1 to 2 tablespoons into sour cream, blending well. Stir back into puree. Season with salt and pepper. Pass sauce separately with palacsintas.

Basic Palacsinta Shells

A creation of Paulette Fono, co-owner with her husband, Laszlo, of the Paprikás Fono restaurant in San Francisco.

10 to 14 shells

3 eggs
1 cup all purpose flour
⅛ teaspoon salt
1 cup milk

½ cup club soda

Oil or butter

Beat eggs in blender on low speed about 10 seconds. Add ½ cup flour with salt and mix again. Add remaining flour with milk and blend well. Transfer to mixing bowl and add soda *(batter should be consistency of whipping cream).*

Heat 7- or 8-inch skillet over medium-high until hot enough that a few drops of water will "dance" on surface. Coat skillet lightly with oil or butter. Add enough batter to cover bottom of pan evenly. Cook until edges of pancake are lightly browned, about 1 minute. Turn and cook other side for 30 seconds. Turn out onto plate and cover with sheet of waxed paper. Repeat with remaining batter, coating pan with oil or butter before cooking each pancake, and stirring through batter before adding to pan. Stack palacsintas between sheets of waxed paper.

Cha Gio (Spring Rolls)

Cha Gio (Spring Rolls) are extremely popular in Vietnam. They are usually filled with pork and crab but any combination of meat, seafood or vegetables can be used. The Vietnamese version of Spring Rolls uses dried rice paper as a wrapper. The rolls can be prepared a day ahead, refrigerated and then fried without becoming soggy. Or they can be cooked ahead and kept warm for up to three hours. They can also be frozen and reheated. Nuoc Cham is used as a dipping sauce.

60 appetizers

Filling
2 tablespoons tree ears (dried oriental mushrooms)
1 cup grated carrot
Salt
1 pound boned and skinned chicken, cut into thin julienne (about 3 cups)
1 medium onion, finely chopped
2 garlic cloves, minced

2 shallots, minced
¼ teaspoon freshly ground pepper

15 dried rice paper wrappers (banh trang), each 12 inches in diameter*
3 eggs, well beaten

Oil
Nuoc Cham (see following recipe)

For filling: Place tree ears in small bowl. Cover with warm water and let stand 30 minutes to soften. Drain well; chop finely and transfer to large bowl.

Place carrot in colander. Sprinkle with salt and let stand several minutes to drain. Squeeze gently to remove excess liquid. Add to tree ears and toss lightly. Add chicken, onion, garlic, shallot and pepper and mix well. Set aside.

Gently cut or fold each wrapper into fourths (they are very brittle and will break easily; any tears can be mended with beaten egg). Paint wrappers thoroughly with egg and let stand several minutes to soften. Spoon 1 teaspoon filling in rectangular shape along curved edge of each wrapper. Roll wrapper once over filling, then fold in sides to enclose. Roll up completely.

Pour oil into skillet to depth of 1 inch. Arrange rolls in single layer in cold oil. Place over medium heat and fry about 10 minutes. Turn rolls and continue frying until golden. Remove from skillet using slotted spoon and drain on paper towels. Serve warm or at room temperature with Nuoc Cham for dipping.

*Rice paper wrappers can be purchased at oriental markets.

Nuoc Cham

No Vietnamese meal is served without this tangy sauce used to add spice to practically everything. It can be refrigerated about 1 week.

Makes about ¾ cup

1 tablespoon plus 2 teaspoons sugar
4 garlic cloves
2 to 4 dried hot chilies or 2 fresh chilies

Juice and pulp of ¼ lime
5 tablespoons water
¼ cup fish sauce (nuoc mam)*

Combine sugar, garlic and chilies in mortar and pound into paste (or mash with back of spoon in mixing bowl). Add lime juice and pulp and continue blending until well mixed. Add water and fish sauce and mix thoroughly.

*Fish sauce (nuoc mam) can be purchased at oriental markets.

 *Meats*

Indonesian Beef Saté

10 servings

Marinade

¼ cup vegetable oil
1 cup finely chopped onion
4 garlic cloves, finely chopped
1 teaspoon grated fresh ginger
¾ cup water
3 tablespoons dark soy sauce
4 teaspoons chili powder

1 tablespoon peanut butter
1 tablespoon turmeric
1 teaspoon brown sugar
½ teaspoon finely grated lemon peel

2 pounds flank steak, sliced crosswise into strips ⅛ inch thick

For marinade: Heat oil in skillet over medium-high heat. Add onion, garlic and ginger and sauté until onion is soft. Add remaining ingredients and stir to make smooth paste. Reduce heat and simmer 2 minutes. Add meat, stirring to coat well. Remove from heat and let stand until room temperature.

Thread meat onto skewers, weaving strips in and out to pack tightly.

Prepare hibachi or barbecue, or preheat broiler. Cook meat 3 to 4 inches from heat source, basting once with any remaining marinade, until crisp and browned, about 3 minutes on each side.

Sirloin Teriyaki

12 servings

1 pound top sirloin, cut into 48 ½-inch cubes
Canned unsweetened mandarin orange sections

¾ cup soy sauce

Alternate 4 pieces of meat with 4 mandarin orange sections on small skewers or bamboo picks. Arrange in single layer in shallow pan. Pour soy sauce over, cover and marinate 1 hour in refrigerator, turning several times. Run under broiler or barbecue to desired doneness. Arrange on serving platter.

Negi Maki (Beef and Scallion Rolls)

A skewered hors d'oeuvre symbolizing strength and eternity.

20 rolls

8 to 10 green onions, trimmed and cut into 2- to 3-inch lengths
½ pound top sirloin (trimmed of fat), sliced paper thin and cut into eight to ten 5 × 2-inch pieces

1 tablespoon vegetable oil or suet
2 tablespoons soy sauce
1 tablespoon sugar

1 tablespoon saké (rice wine)
1 tablespoon Dashi (see recipe, page 51) or water

1 tablespoon mirin (syrupy rice wine)

Divide green onion pieces evenly into 8 to 10 groups. Roll slice of beef snugly around 1 group of onions. Secure with toothpick or tie with string. Repeat with remaining onions and beef.

Heat oil or suet in heavy large skillet over medium-high heat. Add meat rolls seam side down and sauté about 1 minute. Continue sautéing, shaking pan constantly, until rolls are evenly browned. Reduce heat and add soy sauce, sugar, saké and Dashi. Cook another 3 minutes. Remove meat, using slotted spoon, and let cool slightly.

Meanwhile, cook pan juices over medium-high heat until reduced by half. Discard toothpicks or string from rolls. Return rolls to skillet. Add syrupy rice wine and shake pan constantly until well glazed. To serve, cut each roll into ½-inch rounds and thread on skewer. Arrange on serving platter.

Bo Sa Lui (Skewered Beef)

8 servings

4 heaping teaspoons sugar
3 garlic cloves
2 shallots
4 teaspoons fish sauce (nuoc mam)*
4 teaspoons oil
3 stalks fresh lemongrass* (lower bulb portion only), chopped or 3 tablespoons finely chopped dried (soak in hot water 2 hours, then drain and chop)
Freshly ground pepper

1½ pounds top round or sirloin (in 1 piece about 4 inches in diameter), cut into very thin 2 × 2-inch slices

½ package cellophane noodles or rice sticks
2 quarts boiling water
Boston or Bibb lettuce leaves
Carot Chua (see following recipe)
Nuoc Cham (see recipe, page 95)

Combine sugar, garlic and shallots in mortar and pound into paste (or mash with back of spoon in mixing bowl). Add fish sauce, oil, lemongrass and pepper and blend well. Spread on both sides of meat using fingertips. Let stand at room temperature 30 minutes.

Prepare charcoal grill or preheat broiler. Remove any bits of lemongrass clinging to meat. Fold each piece of meat in half and thread about 8 to 10 slices on each skewer. Barbecue or broil until done, turning once, about 3 minutes. Transfer to heated platter and keep warm.

Boil noodles in water 5 minutes. Drain well; rinse under cold water and drain again. Mound noodles on platter next to meat. Arrange lettuce leaves on platter and top with Carot Chua. Serve with Nuoc Cham for dipping.

*Can be purchased at oriental markets.

Carot Chua (Marinated Carrots)

8 servings

2 medium carrots
1 cup water
2 teaspoons vinegar

2 teaspoons sugar
Dash of salt

Cut several wedges lengthwise in each carrot and remove. Slice carrots paper thin (slices should resemble flower petals). Combine all remaining ingredients in small bowl and blend well. Add carrots and mix thoroughly. Let stand 1 hour. Drain well before serving.

Pancakes with Seven Fillings and Sauce

Serve at room temperature.

12 to 14 pancakes

Pancakes
1½ cups all purpose flour
¼ teaspoon salt
2 eggs, beaten
1½ cups milk
1 cup water

Mushroom Filling
20 dried black mushrooms, soaked in boiling water 30 minutes
1 tablespoon vegetable oil
1 tablespoon soy sauce
Dash of sugar
Salt and freshly ground pepper

Egg Filling
3 eggs
Vegetable oil

Meat Filling
1 tablespoon Chinese wine or dry Sherry
2 teaspoons light soy sauce
1 teaspoon dark soy sauce
1 teaspoon cornstarch
1 teaspoon vegetable oil
1 teaspoon hoisin sauce
½ pound flank steak, sliced crosswise into very thin strips

1 tablespoon vegetable oil

Carrot Filling
1 tablespoon vegetable oil
3 carrots, cut into matchsticks
Salt and freshly ground pepper

Onion Filling
1 tablespoon vegetable oil
12 green onions, cut into matchsticks

Daikon Filling
1 tablespoon vegetable oil
1 large daikon (white radish), cut into matchsticks (1 to 1½ cups)
Salt

Zucchini Filling
1 tablespoon vegetable oil
½ pound zucchini, unpeeled, cut into matchsticks
Salt

Sauce
¾ cup soy sauce
3 tablespoons vinegar
3 tablespoons crushed toasted sesame seed
2 tablespoons finely chopped green onion

Vegetable oil

For pancakes: Sift flour and salt into mixing bowl. Combine eggs, milk and water. Add to dry ingredients and beat until smooth. Cover lightly and let stand at room temperature 1 hour.

For mushrooms: Drain mushrooms and squeeze dry, reserving ½ cup liquid. Remove stems and slice caps into thin shreds. Heat oil in large skillet over medium-high heat. Add shredded mushrooms and stir-fry briefly. Add soy sauce, sugar, salt and pepper and reserved liquid. Cover and cook until mushrooms are tender, then uncover and cook until liquid has evaporated. Transfer to serving bowl.

For eggs: Beat eggs. Lightly oil large omelet pan and set over medium heat. Add half of eggs and cook lightly on both sides (do not brown); remove. Cook remaining eggs. When omelets are cool, cut into fine shreds and transfer to another serving bowl.

For meat: Combine wine, soy sauces, cornstarch, 1 teaspoon oil and hoisin in mixing bowl. Add meat and stir well. Marinate for at least 1 hour.

When ready to cook, heat 1 tablespoon oil in wok or skillet over medium-high heat. Add meat and stir-fry until well done. Taste and adjust seasoning. Transfer to serving bowl.

For carrot: Heat oil in large skillet over medium-high heat. Add carrot and stir-fry until crisp-tender. Season with salt and pepper. Transfer to serving bowl.

For onion: Heat oil in large skillet over medium-high heat. Add onion and stir-fry until crisp-tender. Transfer to serving bowl.

For daikon: Heat oil in large skillet over medium-high heat. Add daikon and stir-fry until tender. Season with salt to taste. Transfer to serving bowl.

For zucchini: Heat oil in large skillet over medium-high heat. Add zucchini and cook until tender. Season with salt to taste. Transfer to serving bowl.

For sauce: Mix soy sauce, vinegar, sesame seed and onion in serving bowl.

To cook pancakes: Lightly oil 10-inch skillet (preferably with nonstick finish) and place over low heat. Stir batter; add about ¼ cup to skillet and rotate to spread evenly. Cook until set but not browned; turn and cook on second side. Remove and let cool. Continue until all pancakes are cooked, brushing skillet with oil every 3 or 4 pancakes. Roll each into cylinder and place in serving dish.

Let guests fill pancakes with desired fillings and some of sauce.

Sweet and Sour Meatball Appetizer

32 to 36 meatballs

1 **pound lean ground beef**	1 **teaspoon salt**
¼ **cup water**	⅛ **teaspoon freshly ground pepper**
¼ **cup breadcrumbs**	1 **cup canned chili (without beans)**
1 **egg**	½ **cup grape jelly**
1 **small onion, grated**	**Juice of 1 lemon**

Combine first 7 ingredients and blend well. Shape into 1-inch meatballs. Combine remaining ingredients in medium saucepan and mix well. Add meatballs, stirring lightly to coat with sauce. Simmer about 1 hour, stirring occasionally.

Mini Swedish Meatballs

6 servings

2 **teaspoons butter or margarine**	1 **small egg**
2 **tablespoons minced onion**	**Pinch of nutmeg**
½ **cup mashed potatoes**	2 **tablespoons butter or margarine**
¼ **cup fine breadcrumbs**	1 **tablespoon vegetable oil**
½ **pound lean ground chuck**	1 **tablespoon instant flour**
¾ **cup whipping cream**	
Salt	

Melt butter and sauté onion until pale gold. Remove from heat.

Combine mashed potatoes, breadcrumbs, meat, ¼ cup cream, salt, egg, nutmeg and sautéed onion. Mix until light and well blended. Shape mixture into ¾-inch balls and chill.

When ready to cook, heat butter and oil in a large skillet. Fry meatballs over medium heat, shaking the pan so that all sides are browned. Keep warm.

Over high heat, sprinkle flour into the skillet juices, blend, and add remaining cream, stirring until mixture thickens slightly. Pour over meatballs. Serve hot.

Veal Meatballs

60 meatballs

⅔ pound ground veal
3 sweet Italian sausages, casings removed (about 12 ounces)
3 ¾-inch slices stale Italian bread, moistened and squeezed dry
2 eggs
¼ cup freshly grated Parmesan cheese
3 tablespoons minced fresh parsley
½ teaspoon salt
¼ teaspoon freshly grated nutmeg
  Freshly ground pepper

1 cup very fine stale white breadcrumbs
  Olive oil
  Lemon slices
  Parsley sprigs
  Cherry tomatoes
  Caper Mayonnaise (see following recipe)

Combine veal, sausage, Italian bread, eggs, Parmesan, parsley, salt, nutmeg and freshly ground pepper in processor and mix using on/off turns just until well combined; *do not overprocess.* Refrigerate at least 1 hour.

   Shape mixture into 1-inch balls. Roll in crumbs. Pour olive oil into heavy large skillet to depth of ½ inch and heat over medium-high heat until very hot (400°F). Add meatballs in batches and fry until golden on all sides, about 5 minutes. Remove with slotted spoon and drain on paper towels. *(Meatballs can be prepared ahead and kept warm in 200°F oven for 30 minutes.)* Arrange on platter. Garnish with lemon slices, parsley and tomatoes. Pass mayonnaise separately.

Caper Mayonnaise

Makes about 2 cups

1½ cups olive oil
2 egg yolks, room temperature
1 tablespoon fresh lemon juice

2 tablespoons capers, well drained
1 to 2 tablespoons anchovy paste
  Salt and freshly ground pepper

Combine 3 tablespoons olive oil, egg yolks and lemon juice in processor. Blend using on/off turns until mixture thickens slightly. With machine running, pour remaining oil through feed tube in thin stream (mayonnaise will thicken as oil is added). Stir in capers and 1 tablespoon anchovy paste. Taste and add remaining anchovy paste if desired. Season with salt and pepper.

Frikadeller (Danish Meatballs)

4 servings

½ pound veal
½ pound pork
½ cup milk
1 egg
1 teaspoon salt

  Freshly ground pepper
1 medium onion, grated
6 tablespoons flour or ½ cup breadcrumbs
6 tablespoons (¾ stick) butter

Grind veal and pork together through grinder 4 or 5 times. Add next 6 ingredients and mix thoroughly. Heat half of butter in skillet over low heat. Drop meat mixture from large tablespoon and cook, turning often, until desired doneness, about 15 to 20 minutes. Remove and keep warm. Repeat with remaining butter and meat mixture.

   Frikadeller are served with browned butter, potatoes and stewed cabbage.

Saté Babi (Skewered Barbecued Pork)

18 servings

1 small onion, chopped
1 piece fresh ginger (about 1 inch long), peeled and minced
1 garlic clove, minced
½ cup Indonesian soy sauce or Kecap Manis (see recipe, following page)

2 tablespoons fresh lime juice
1 pound lean, boneless pork, cut into ½-inch cubes

Kacang Saus (see recipe, page 103)

Combine onion, ginger, garlic, soy sauce and lime juice in bowl. Add pork and mix well. Cover and marinate 2 hours, tossing occasionally with fork.

Prepare charcoal (or use broiler). Remove pork from marinade and thread on wooden or bamboo skewers (5 or 6 cubes to each 6- to 8-inch skewer). Grill or broil satés slowly, turning frequently and basting with marinade, until done, about 8 to 10 minutes. Serve with Kacang Saus for dipping.

Piquant Fruit-Glazed Ribs with Orange Slices

These ribs develop a rich, crusty glaze, but stay moist on the inside.

8 servings

4 quarts water
1 pound onions, halved
4 garlic cloves, halved
2 tablespoons salt
2 pounds pork back ribs (have butcher split each rack of ribs lengthwise so rib bones are 2 to 2½ inches long)

Glaze
¾ cup fresh or canned unsweetened pineapple chunks, pureed
¾ cup sugar
¾ cup cider vinegar

¼ cup plus 2 tablespoons dark soy sauce
2 medium garlic cloves, minced
2 tablespoons frozen orange juice concentrate
1 tablespoon finely grated orange peel
¾ teaspoon dry mustard
¾ teaspoon ground ginger
¼ cup Scotch whisky

1 orange, scored and thinly sliced (garnish)
Parsley sprigs (garnish)

Combine water, onion, garlic and salt and bring to boil. Add ribs and simmer uncovered 25 minutes.

Meanwhile, combine all ingredients for glaze except whisky and simmer 5 minutes. Blend in whisky and simmer an additional 2 minutes.

Drain ribs thoroughly. Leave in pan and immediately pour hot glaze evenly over them. Transfer to container just large enough to accommodate; cover and chill 24 hours, basting occasionally.

Just before serving time, preheat oven to 400°F. Line baking sheet with foil. Arrange ribs rounded side down on foil, making sure they are still coated with glaze. Bake 25 minutes. Turn ribs over, brush with remaining glaze and bake until deeply colored, about 5 to 10 minutes. Separate ribs with kitchen shears and arrange in shallow dish. Garnish with orange slices and parsley.

Lamb Meatballs

45 meatballs

2 tablespoons (¼ stick) unsalted butter
5 shallots, minced
2 pounds ground lamb
1 cup fresh breadcrumbs
¼ cup chopped fresh parsley
1 egg, lightly beaten

2 tablespoons finely grated lemon peel
½ teaspoon ground marjoram
Salt and freshly ground pepper

1 tablespoon unsalted butter
1 tablespoon olive oil

Melt 2 tablespoons butter in small skillet over medium heat. Add shallot and sauté until softened. Transfer to large bowl and add lamb, breadcrumbs, parsley, egg, lemon peel, marjoram, salt and pepper and blend well. Form into balls about the size of chestnuts.

Heat remaining butter with oil in large skillet over medium-high heat. Add meatballs in batches and sauté until browned on all sides and cooked as desired. Drain on paper towels. Reheat in low oven before serving.

Saté Kambing (Skewered Barbecued Lamb)

12 servings

3 large green onions, minced
1 large garlic clove, minced
½ cup Indonesian soy sauce or Kecap Manis (see following recipe)
1 tablespoon fresh lemon juice
½ teaspoon sambal oelek* (crushed chili paste), crushed red pepper flakes or chili powder

1 pound boneless lean lamb shoulder, cut into ½-inch cubes
Kacang Saus (see recipe, opposite page)

Combine onion, garlic, soy sauce, lemon juice and seasoning in bowl. Add lamb and mix well. Cover and marinate 1 hour, tossing frequently. Broil, turning and basting, about 5 minutes, or until done. Serve with Kacang Saus.

*Can be purchased at Indonesian markets.

Kecap Manis (Indonesian Soy Sauce)

A common ingredient in Balinese and Indonesian cuisine similar to soy sauce. If commercial Kecap Manis is not readily available, use this recipe.

Makes about 3 cups

1 cup firmly packed dark brown sugar
1 cup water
1 cup Japanese soy sauce

7 tablespoons dark molasses
1 teaspoon grated fresh ginger
½ teaspoon ground coriander
½ teaspoon freshly ground pepper

Combine sugar and water in 2-quart saucepan. Bring to simmer over medium heat, stirring just until sugar dissolves. Increase heat to high and continue cooking until syrup reaches 200°F on candy thermometer, about 5 minutes. Reduce heat to low, stir in remaining ingredients and simmer 3 minutes.

Kecap Manis will keep 2 to 3 months tightly covered and refrigerated.

Kacang Saus (Peanut Sauce)

Makes about 2 cups

1½ cups salted Spanish peanuts with skins (not dry-roasted) or peanut butter

1 tablespoon peanut oil
¼ cup chopped onion
4 garlic cloves, minced
1½ cups coconut milk* or canned coconut cream
1½ to 2 teaspoons sambal oelek** (crushed chili paste), crushed red pepper flakes or chili powder

1 teaspoon ground ginger
¼ teaspoon ground cumin
3 tablespoons fresh lemon juice
4 to 5 tablespoons Indonesian soy sauce or Kecap Manis (see preceding recipe)

Place peanuts in processor or blender and mix to paste or butter, stopping to scrape down sides as necessary.

Heat oil in small saucepan. Add onion and garlic and sauté about 1 minute. Stirring constantly, add coconut milk, sambal oelek, ginger, cumin, lemon juice and soy sauce or Kecap Manis and bring to boil. Whisk in peanut butter and cook, stirring constantly, until sauce is thickened, about 3 to 5 minutes.

*The coconut milk called for in this recipe is not the liquid from a fresh coconut, but milk and the essential oils and flavors extracted from coconut meat. In Indonesia it is called *santen,* which translates to coconut cream. To make 2½ cups, combine 3 cups packaged, flaked coconut and 3 cups milk in blender. Do not blend. Refrigerate for 1½ hours. Whirl mixture at low speed 30 seconds. Strain through sieve lined with double thickness of cheesecloth that has been dampened and wrung out. Press and squeeze until all liquid has been extracted.

**Can be purchased at Indonesian markets.

Butterflied Leg of Lamb

25 servings

Pomegranate Marinade
4 large onions, cut into chunks
4 garlic cloves
2 cups pomegranate juice
1 cup dry red wine
1 lemon, unpeeled and cut into chunks
4 teaspoons basil leaves

1 tablespoon salt
1 teaspoon freshly ground pepper

2 8-pound legs of lamb, trimmed and butterflied

For marinade: Combine all ingredients in processor or blender (in batches if necessary) and puree.

Arrange lamb in two 10 × 14-inch roasting pans. Pour half of marinade over top of each leg of lamb, turning lamb to cover completely. Marinate 8 to 10 hours at room temperature or chill 1 to 2 days.

Preheat broiler. Wipe excess marinade from lamb. Arrange in pan and broil 5 to 6 inches from heat source, turning frequently to brown evenly (inside should be pink), about 30 to 35 minutes. Slice thinly to serve.

Lamb can also be barbecued.

Siu Mai (Steamed Meat Dumplings)

60 appetizers

Dumplings
- 1 pound ground pork or ½ pound ground pork and ½ pound ground pork sausage
- ¼ cup chicken broth
- ¼ cup cornstarch
- ¼ cup minced Chinese parsley (also called cilantro)
- 8 water chestnuts (about ½ of 8-ounce can), diced
- 4 dried mushrooms, soaked, squeezed dry and minced
- 1 green onion, minced
- 2 tablespoons sugar
- 1 tablespoon minced fresh ginger
- 1 tablespoon light soy sauce
- 1 teaspoon salt
- ½ teaspoon teriyaki sauce
- ½ teaspoon Sherry
- ½ teaspoon sesame oil
- 60 won ton skins
  Soy-Sesame Dip (see following recipe)

Combine all ingredients except won ton skins and Soy-Sesame Dip in large bowl and blend well. With scissors, trim corners from skins to make circles. Spoon about 1 teaspoon of mixture into center of circle, gather up sides and let dough "pleat" naturally. Flatten filling slightly with thumb and gently tap bottom on flat surface so dumpling will stand upright.

Arrange dumplings in aluminum steamer and steam 15 to 20 minutes. Serve hot with dip.

Dumplings may be prepared ahead. Steam, cool, wrap tightly and freeze. To serve, resteam 15 to 20 minutes.

Soy-Sesame Dip

Makes about ¼ cup

- 3 tablespoons light soy sauce
- 1 teaspoon vinegar
- 1 teaspoon sesame oil

Combine all ingredients and mix well.

Pot Stickers

40 appetizers

- ⅔ pound ground pork
- 1 cup minced cabbage
- 2 green onions, minced
- 1 egg
- 1 tablespoon light soy sauce
- ½ teaspoon salt
- ½ teaspoon grated orange peel (optional)
- ½ teaspoon hot chili oil (optional)*
- Cornstarch
- 40 won ton skins, each cut into largest circle possible
- ½ cup peanut oil
- 1 cup water
  Hot chili oil*
  Chinese vinegar or white wine vinegar or red wine vinegar

Combine pork, cabbage, onion, egg, soy sauce, salt, orange peel and hot chili oil in large bowl and mix well.

To assemble: Dust waxed or parchment paper with cornstarch. Set 1 rounded teaspoon filling in center of won ton skin, pressing lightly so filling forms narrow band across middle. Moisten rim of skin. Bring opposite sides together to form semicircle. Pinch corners together. Seal remainder by pleating one side 3 to 4 times and pressing against opposite (unpleated) side. Tap lightly on bottom if necessary so dumpling stands upright. Transfer to cornstarch-dusted paper. Cover with dry kitchen towel. Repeat with remaining won ton and filling.

Place 2 heavy 12-inch skillets over low heat. Add ¼ cup oil to each. Arrange dumplings in skillets in rows, fitting closely together. Increase heat to medium-high and cook uncovered until bottoms are deeply golden, about 2 minutes, checking occasionally.

Add ½ cup water to each pan and cover immediately. Let steam until skins are translucent, about 3 minutes. Remove cover and continue cooking over medium to medium-high heat until bottoms are very crisp and well browned. Drain off excess oil if necessary. Loosen dumplings with spatula and transfer to serving dish. Serve immediately with chili oil and vinegar.

Pot Stickers can be assembled ahead and frozen. Do not dust waxed or parchment paper with cornstarch before shaping. Defrost completely before frying and steaming.

*Can be purchased at oriental markets.

Szekely Goulash

A hearty dish that can be served as part of a hot appetizer buffet or as a main course.

12 main-course or 24 buffet servings

3 strips bacon, chopped and blanched*
1 tablespoon butter
3 large onions, chopped
3½ to 4 tablespoons Hungarian paprika (sweet or medium type)
3 pounds lean pork from shoulder, butt or rib, cut into small chunks
2¼ cups beef broth (do not use bouillon cubes)

3 pounds sauerkraut, rinsed and drained
3 tablespoons tomato paste
¾ teaspoon caraway seed
  Salt and freshly ground pepper
  Sour cream (garnish)

Heat bacon and butter in heavy 4- to 5-quart casserole over medium heat. When bacon begins to brown, remove with slotted spoon. Increase heat to medium-high, add onion and cook until golden brown. Reduce heat to low, stir in paprika and cook briefly, stirring constantly. Add pork and toss to combine well. Add broth, cover and simmer about 1 hour, or until pork is barely tender.

Stir in sauerkraut, reserved bacon, tomato paste and caraway seed; cover and cook 30 minutes, or until pork is tender, adding more broth if mixture seems dry. Season to taste with salt and pepper. Refrigerate until ready to serve. Pass sour cream separately.

Can be prepared 3 to 4 days before serving or frozen for up to a month.

*To blanch chopped bacon, bring 2 cups water to a boil, add bacon and boil 2 to 3 minutes. Drain well and pat dry between paper towels. Blanching removes most of the fat and salt and tones down the smoky taste of the bacon.

Crespelle with Italian Sausage and Salsa Balsamella

12 to 24 servings

Crespelle Batter
- 1 cup all purpose flour
- 2 cups milk, room temperature
- 3 eggs
- 1 egg yolk
- 1 teaspoon salt
- ¼ teaspoon freshly ground pepper
- ⅛ teaspoon freshly grated nutmeg

- ¼ cup (½ stick) butter, melted and cooled

Filling
- 1 cup milk
- 1 ounce dried Italian mushrooms

- 2 tablespoons (¼ stick) butter
- 1 small onion, minced

- 1 pound luganega* or other sweet, finely ground Italian sausage (casing removed)

Salsa Balsamella
- 2½ to 3 cups milk
- 6 tablespoons (¾ stick) butter
- 6 tablespoons all purpose flour

- 1 cup whipping cream
- 3 egg yolks

- 3 ounces freshly grated imported Parmesan cheese
- Salt and freshly ground pepper
- Freshly grated nutmeg

- 1 tablespoon butter

For crespelle: Place flour in large bowl. Pour in ⅔ cup milk, a little at a time, whisking constantly to make smooth paste. Gradually whisk in remaining 1⅓ cups milk, eggs, egg yolk, salt, pepper and nutmeg. Let stand at room temperature about 1 hour.

Press batter through sieve to remove any lumps. Stir in butter. Lightly oil 8-inch nonstick fry pan and place over medium-high heat. When almost smoking, remove pan from heat and ladle about 3 tablespoons batter into one corner of pan, then tilt pan and swirl until bottom is covered with thin layer of batter. Pour any excess batter back into mixing bowl.

Return pan to medium-high heat, loosen edges of crespelle with small spatula or knife and cook until bottom is brown, shaking pan in a circle to prevent sticking, about 1 minute. Turn crespelle over with spatula and cook until second side is brown, about 1 minute. Slide out onto plate. Repeat procedure until all batter is used, oiling pan after every two or three crespelle. *(Crespelle can be made ahead. Let cool, wrap in plastic and refrigerate up to 3 to 4 days or wrap tightly in foil and freeze.)*

For filling: Scald milk in small saucepan. Remove from heat, add mushrooms and let stand about 30 minutes to soften. Drain mushrooms well; reserve milk for Salsa Balsamella.

Heat butter in medium skillet over low heat. Add onion, cover and cook until translucent, about 15 minutes. Add sausage, crumbling with fork. Add reserved mushrooms and cook until meat is just brown, stirring frequently, about 10 minutes. Drain any excess fat. Transfer sausage mixture to medium bowl.

For Salsa Balsamella: Measure reserved milk and add enough additional milk to equal 3 cups. Melt butter in heavy 2-quart saucepan over medium-low heat. Add flour and cook, whisking constantly, for 3 minutes. Gradually whisk in milk. Increase heat and cook, stirring constantly until sauce boils and thickens. Reduce heat and simmer 5 minutes. Remove from heat.

Mix cream and egg yolks in small bowl. Slowly stir 1 cup sauce into mixture, then whisk back into remaining sauce.

To assemble: Butter 9 × 12-inch baking dish. Add 2 cups sauce to sausage mixture and blend well. Stir in 2 ounces Parmesan cheese. Season to taste with salt, pepper and nutmeg.

Spread several tablespoons of filling over lower edge of least attractive side of crespelle. Fold ¼ inch of edge over filling, then roll up crepe fashion. Set seam side down in prepared dish. Repeat with remaining crespelle.

Season remaining cup of sauce with salt, pepper and nutmeg. Spoon over crespelle, covering completely. Sprinkle with remaining cheese and dot with 1 tablespoon butter. *(Crespelle and sauce can be made several days ahead to this point, covered and refrigerated. Bring to room temperature before baking.)*

Preheat oven to 400°F. Bake crespelle until heated through and sauce is bubbly, about 15 minutes. Broil 1 minute to brown cheese lightly.

*Available at Italian delicatessens.

Spanish Sausage

6 servings

1 garlic clove, finely minced
1 tablespoon olive oil
1 pound spicy Spanish sausage, cut into thin rounds

¼ teaspoon ground coriander
½ cup dry red Rioja wine

Sauté garlic in olive oil until golden. Add sausage and brown lightly. Add coriander and wine. Simmer until liquid is slightly thickened. Serve either hot or cold.

Carnitas

6 servings

3 corn tortillas
Vegetable oil

1 cup shredded or chopped roast pork
1 teaspoon chili powder

Salt
1 small tomato, peeled, seeded and diced
Shredded lettuce (garnish)

With round cookie cutter, cut 4 small tortillas from each large one. Heat enough oil to cover bottom of large skillet and partially cook tortillas on both sides. Fold in half in pan and continue frying until almost crisp. Remove tortillas and drain on paper towels.

Brown pork in same skillet, adding chili powder and salt to taste. Remove from heat and stir in tomato. Stuff tortillas with the mixture. Serve warm or cold on bed of shredded lettuce.

Korean Mondu

12 servings

3 cabbage leaves
Salt

½ bunch green onions
1 pound ground pork
½ pound lean ground beef
1 garlic clove, pressed
1 1½-inch piece peeled ginger
1½ teaspoons sugar

1 teaspoon salt

1 package won ton wrappers
1 egg white, lightly beaten

Peanut oil

Boiling water (3 to 6 cups)

Sprinkle cabbage leaves lightly with salt and set aside 5 minutes. Chop finely. Squeeze out all liquid with paper towels and transfer cabbage to mixing bowl.

Chop green onions in processor or by hand, using all but top 3 inches of stem. Add to cabbage along with pork, beef and garlic. Fit ginger into garlic press and squeeze liquid into meat mixture; add ⅛ teaspoon of the pulp (discard remainder). Blend in sugar and salt.

Working with 4 won ton wrappers at a time (keep remainder lightly covered to prevent drying), spoon 1 teaspoon meat mixture into center of each. Fold in half, sealing edges with egg white.

Heat 2 tablespoons oil in large deep skillet with lid. Arrange mondu with sides touching in hot oil. Fry uncovered until bottom is golden brown. Set baking sheet over skillet and invert carefully. Return skillet to heat and slide mondu back into pan. Fry on second side until golden. Remove. Repeat with remaining mondu, adding oil as needed.

Leave last mondu in skillet and reduce heat. Carefully add about 1 cup boiling water *(it will spatter)*. Cover skillet and cook over medium heat until all water is absorbed, checking to make sure dough is not sticking to pan (adjust heat as needed). Repeat with boiling water, if necessary, until mondu is crisp and cooked through. Transfer to heated platter and keep warm. Repeat to finish remaining mondu. Serve immediately.

Mondu can be made ahead and reheated until crisp in 375°F oven.

Mondu can also be served in chicken soup. Simmer uncovered (steam will cause the mondu to pop open) until cooked through.

6 ❦ Drinks

Fashions in entertaining, like fashions in anything else, are subject to enormous periodic changes. One social institution that has seen a lot of change in recent years is the cocktail party. For decades, invitations to pre-dinner gatherings invariably read, "Come for cocktails," and what was served was pretty much as advertised: mixed drinks or, during the holiday season, some sort of festive punch. Food played a decidedly secondary role, and usually consisted of cheese and crackers or peanuts.

Cocktail parties have not vanished, of course, but the emphasis has shifted almost 180 degrees. With the great explosion of interest in cooking, it is now often as not the food, in the form of appetizers, that is the focus. In place of mixed drinks, wine is likely to be offered—logically enough, since it can be argued that wine is more compatible with food, and pouring wine is also easier than mixing drinks.

Fashions aside, there are no ironclad rules about what beverages should be served with appetizers; the only important guideline is that whatever is offered should truly complement the food. Wine is certainly a safe choice, though it should be chosen with careful attention to the appetizers being served (see box, page 110). But appropriate cocktails and punches, particularly the light, refreshing combinations on the following pages, can give an appetizer party a flair that, like any classic fashion, is timeless.

🍷 Wines with Appetizers

Hors d'oeuvres come in many varieties and so do the wines that accompany them. A good solution is to serve a well-chilled *fino* Sherry, especially with a large variety of canapés and appetizers. If you are serving caviar, Champagne is the ticket and if you offer *foie gras* or pâté the choice should be, surprisingly enough, a sweet French Sauternes. If you include quiche, crab or shrimp, serve white French Burgundies, wines from the German Rheingau, California Chardonnay (current favorites include versions by Grgich Hills, Beringer, Chateau St. Jean, Zaca Mesa, Sterling, Robert Mondavi, Raymond, Chateau Montelena, Cuvaison, Robert Keenan, Ventana, Alexander Valley Vineyards, Burgess, Hacienda, Jekel, Joseph Phelps and Pendleton), California Riesling (look for Jekel, Chateau St. Jean or Joseph Phelps) or Gewürztraminer (try Hacienda, Parducci, Chateau St. Jean, Clos du Bois, Grand Cru and Landmark).

Charcuterie works best with the same young red wines that show an affinity for turkey, but cheeses need to be individually matched with wines. A good basic rule of thumb is to select a wine that comes from the same area that produced the cheese. For example, Fontina with Barolo, Roquefort with Bordeaux (Sauternes is also marvelous) or Monterey Jack with Zinfandel. There are other cheese and wine combinations that are traditional such as Stilton with Port but, in general, the best way to deal with a selection of cheese is to offer a choice of wines that is just as varied. Let your guests experiment with different pairings.

Champagne Framboise

A simple aperitif that can be adapted for any number of guests.

8 servings

1 16-ounce can whole raspberries in heavy syrup

Framboise
Chilled Champagne

Divide raspberries and syrup among ice cube trays and freeze solidly. Place 1 cube in each of 8 Champagne or other stemmed glasses. Add 1 to 3 teaspoons Framboise to each glass and fill with Champagne. Serve immediately.

Kir Royale with Raspberries

16 to 24 servings

1 cup raspberries
¼ cup crème de cassis

2 to 3 bottles brut Champagne, well chilled

For each serving, place 2 to 3 raspberries in Champagne glass. Add ½ teaspoon crème de cassis to each. Pour Champagne over and serve.

Planter's Punch

1 serving

3 ounces (¼ cup plus 2 tablespoons) dark rum
2 teaspoons fresh lime juice
1 teaspoon brown sugar
Dash of Angostura bitters

Several drops of grenadine
Club soda (optional)
Lime slice and maraschino cherry (garnish)

Fill tall glass ¾ full with shaved ice and set aside in freezer. Combine rum, lime juice, sugar, bitters and grenadine in cocktail shaker or jar filled with ice cubes and shake until sugar is dissolved. Strain into glass. Top off with soda if desired. Garnish with lime slice and maraschino cherry and serve.

Margarita Punch

50 servings

3 quarts tequila
4 cups (1 quart) Triple Sec
2 cups fresh lemon juice
2 cups fresh lime juice

Block of ice
2 quarts club soda
Coarse salt
Fresh lime wedges

Combine tequila, Triple Sec, lemon juice and lime juice in large bowl, blending well. Refrigerate. Shortly before serving, place block of ice in large punch bowl. Add tequila mixture and soda and stir gently until blended. Pour salt into saucer. Run lime wedges around rims of punch cups, then press rims into salt. Ladle punch into salt-rimmed cups and serve.

Bengal Lancers' Punch

50 servings

2 1.5-liter bottles good red wine
  (such as Cabernet Sauvignon)
3 cups fresh orange juice
1½ cups light rum
1½ cups fresh lemon or lime juice
1½ cups Triple Sec

Block of ice
2 bottles Champagne or sparkling wine
4 cups (1 quart) club soda
Fresh strawberries (garnish)

Combine red wine, orange juice, rum, lemon or lime juice and Triple Sec in large bowl, blending well. Refrigerate. Shortly before serving, place block of ice in large punch bowl. Add red wine mixture, Champagne and club soda and stir gently until blended. Garnish with fresh strawberries.

Daiquiri

One of the classic rum cocktails.

1 serving

1½ ounces (3 tablespoons) white rum
1 teaspoon Triple Sec

1 teaspoon superfine sugar
Juice of ½ lime

Combine all ingredients in cocktail shaker or jar filled with ice cubes and shake until sugar is dissolved. Strain into chilled cocktail glass and serve.

Minted Rye Punch

35 servings

2 quarts rock and rye (or 1½ quarts rye whiskey and 1 cup sugar dissolved in 1 cup water)
2 cups sweet Italian vermouth
1 cup fresh lemon juice

Block of ice
3 quarts ginger ale
Fresh mint leaves (garnish)

Combine rock and rye, vermouth and lemon juice in large bowl, blending well. Refrigerate. Shortly before serving, place block of ice in punch bowl. Add rock and rye mixture and ginger ale and stir gently until blended. Garnish with mint.

🍎 Party Punch Tips

When it is your turn to host a holiday get-together you will, obviously, have to concern yourself with what to offer people to drink. Unless you are eager to tend bar all night or plan to hire a bartender, the best solution is a cold refreshing punch or, if the icy winds are particularly fierce, a hot concoction served up in steaming mugs. But certain rules and procedures must be followed to ensure a successful party.

For a cold punch you'll need a punch bowl and plenty of cups. If you don't own this equipment, you can usually rent it or borrow it from a friend. Just be sure that the punch bowl you use is big enough to accommodate a large block of ice.

When making punches or hot drinks, don't skimp on ingredients. Use mixers, wines and spirits of the best quality. Try to use fresh fruit juices if possible. If you do use frozen concentrate, dilute it with only half as much water as is called for on the label. Follow recipes carefully. If a recipe specifies a medium Barbados rum, for example, use a good one such as Mount Gay, not just any rum you happen to have in your liquor cabinet.

The secret of great mixed drinks is to make sure that no individual ingredient dominates the others. All elements should blend perfectly to make a special new taste. To achieve this marriage of ingredients it is important to combine them in the order and according to the method prescribed by the particular punch recipe.

Dilution from melting ice can be a problem with cold punches, but this can be minimized in several ways. First of all, the punch can be mixed in advance—all ingredients except perishable items such as Champagne or carbonated mixers—and rebottled in the empty liquor and wine bottles or other containers. (It is always desirable to blend punch at least one hour in advance to let the flavors mix thoroughly.) Preblending allows you to use a bottle or two at a time while the rest of the punch remains, undiluted, to be used later or another day.

Another way to fight dilution is to make your own ice block and, if you are using it with a punch that contains fruit juice, to make the ice out of the same fruit juice. Use your favorite gelatin mold to make a prettily shaped block. You can even freeze strawberries, cherries or grapes in the mold for a special visual surprise.

All ingredients for cold punches should be well chilled before preparation begins. And hot drinks must be served hot, not lukewarm. When you are gauging how much punch to make, figure at least two four-ounce servings per person. Most punch recipes can be halved, doubled or multiplied by any number you like. Just be sure to multiply each ingredient.

Sidney Blue's Brighton Punch

24 servings

1 block of ice
1 750-ml bottle Sidney Blue's Brighton Punch Base (see following recipe)
6½ ounces (¾ cup plus 1 tablespoon) fresh lemon juice

1 quart or 1 liter club soda
Orange slices (garnish)

Set ice in large bowl and pour punch base over top. Add lemon juice and club soda and mix gently. Float orange slices on top for garnish.

Sidney Blue's Brighton Punch Base

2 1.5-liter bottles dark rum
1 750-ml bottle medium rum
1 750-ml bottle light rum

1 750-ml bottle apricot brandy
12 ounces (1½ cups) Falernum

Combine all ingredients in stockpot or other large container and blend thoroughly. Pour mixture back into empty rum bottles to store.

Hot Mulled Cider

8 servings

4½ cups (36 ounces) apple cider or juice
1 small orange wedge (about ⅙ orange)

1 cinnamon stick
¾ cup (6 ounces) rum
¾ cup (6 ounces) applejack

Combine cider, orange and cinnamon stick in saucepan. Warm over low heat until mixture begins to simmer. Remove from heat. Stir in rum and applejack. Pour into heated mugs and serve immediately.

Wassail

This is an adaptation of the English holiday favorite.

20 servings

1 cup sugar
½ cup water
3 lemon slices
2 cinnamon sticks
1 pint (2 cups) cranberry juice

1 pint (2 cups) fresh, frozen or bottled lemon juice
1 quart (4 cups) red wine
Lemon slices (garnish)

Boil first 4 ingredients in small saucepan for about 5 minutes. Strain syrup into small bowl or measuring cup. Combine cranberry and lemon juices and red wine in large saucepan and bring to simmer. Remove from heat and stir in syrup. Serve immediately garnished with lemon slices.

🌿 Index

Anchovies
  Anchovy Puffs, 63
  Crostino Caldo alla Re Guido
    d'Andrea, 71
  Roasted Stuffed Peppers with
    Anchovies, 87
  Snow Peas with Lemon-Anchovy
    Dipping Sauce, 3
Angel of Death Cheese, 5
Armenian Pizza, 66
Artichokes
  Artichoke and Chestnut Pâté, 9
  Artichoke Bottoms with Pâté, 22
  Artichoke Hearts with Sauce
    Rémoulade, 32
  Artichoke Tree, 33
Asparagus
  Asparagus Cheese Fritters, 82
  Mini-Crepes with Asparagus, 56
Aspic
  Aspic for Glazing, Molding and
    Garnishing, 30
  Duck Liver Pâté in Port Aspic, 23
  Fish Aspic, 20
  Stock-Based Aspic, 30
  Striped Bass Mold with Vegetable
    Floral Design, 20
  Stuffed Veal Roll with Hazelnuts
    in Aspic, 43
  Tomato Aspic with Water
    Chestnuts, 29
  Tomato-Herb Aspic, 13
Avocado
  Avocado and Radish Mousse with
    Radish Pompons, 13
  Avocado Gazpacho Mold, 32
  Avocado-Yogurt Dip, 2
  Perfect Guacamole, 4
  Shrimp Mousse with Avocado
    Surprise, 21
  Squid, Fennel and Avocado Salad,
    35

Baked Brie Spread, 7
Baked Mushrooms, 83
Barquettes, Filled, 61
Basic Palacsinta Shells, 94
Basic Sourdough Starter, 75
Basic Stock, 51
Beans
  Garbanzo-Sesame Spread, 8
  Refritos, 8
  White Bean and Zucchini Pâté, 10
  White Bean Shrimp Salad, 36
Beef
  Bo Sa Lui (Skewered Beef), 97
  Carpaccio (Italian Beef Appetizer),
    42
  Chinese Beef Jerky, 57
  Indonesian Beef Saté, 96
  Kreatopetes (Spicy Meat-Stuffed
    Appetizers), 64
  Lahmajoon (Armenian Pizza), 66
  Mini Swedish Meatballs, 99
  Negi Maki (Beef and Scallion
    Rolls), 96
  Sirloin Teriyaki, 96
  Siu Mai (Steamed Meat
    Dumplings), 104
  Sweet and Sour Meatball
    Appetizer, 99
Beets
  Beet Salad, 29
  Herring-Stuffed Beets, 56
Belgian Endive with Bleu Cheese, 55
Bengal Lancers' Punch, 111
Beverages
  Champagne Framboise, 110
  Daiquiri, 111
  Hot Mulled Cider, 113
  Kir Royale with Raspberries, 110
  Wassail, 113
  See also Punches
Bird's Nest, 35
Bleu Cheese Log, 6
Bo Sa Lui (Skewered Beef, 97

Breads
  Crusty French Bread, 74
  Crusty Whole Wheat Bread, 76
  Emerald Isle Bread, 77
  Finger Biscuits, 45
  Hors d'Oeuvre Biscuits, 79
  Pesto Pizza Bread, 77
  Quick Brown Bread, 76
  Sandwich Bread, 73
  Sourdough French Bread, 74
  Sourdough Whole Wheat Bread,
    75
  Whole Wheat Ballons, 78
Brie Spread, Baked, 7
Butterflied Leg of Lamb, 103

Canapés
  A Canapé Primer, 69
  Curried Chicken-Almond
    Canapés, 68
  Mozzarella-Tomato Canapés, 68
  Parmesan Rounds, 70
  Turkish Bread Rounds with
    Mediterranean Zucchini Salad,
    70
Cantonese Stuffed Chicken Wings,
  93
Caper Mayonnaise, 100
Caponata (Italian Eggplant
  Appetizer), 7
Carnitas, 107
Carpaccio (Italian Beef Appetizer),
  42
Carrots
  Carot Chua (Marinated Carrots),
    97
  Carrot and Spinach Striped Pâté,
    12
  Cauliflower, Carrot and Squash
    Salad, 28
Cauliflower
  Cauliflower, Carrot and Squash
    Salad, 28

Cauliflower *(continued)*
    Marinated Cauliflower, 53
Caviar
    Buying and Serving, 18
    Caviar Mousse, 18
    Caviar Ring, 19
Ceviche, 38
Cha Gio (Spring Rolls), 95
Champagne Framboise, 110
Chang's Anise-Smoked Duck, 42
Cheese
    Angel of Death Cheese, 5
    Asparagus Cheese Fritters, 82
    Baked Brie Salad, 7
    Belgian Endive with Bleu Cheese,
      55
    Bleu Cheese Log, 6
    Cheese Whole Wheat Short Pastry
      Tartlet Shells, 61
    Chile con Queso, 2
    Cream Cheese and Almond
      Tartlets, 60
    Crostino Caldo alla Re Guido
      d'Andrea, 71
    Deep-Fried Cheese, 88
    Filled Tartlets, 60
    Foglie de Salvia Ripiene, 88
    Grapes Stuffed with Bleu Cheese,
      55
    Herb Dip, 2
    Homemade Herb Cheese, 7
    Hot Mushroom-Filled Cheese
      Puffs, 63
    Liptauer Cheese, 6
    Mozzarella-Tomato Canapés, 68
    Parmesan Rounds, 70
    Puff Pastry Palm Leaves with
      Cheese, 62
    Queso, 89
    Sesame Cheese Crisps, 80
    Spiced Cheese-Stuffed Pepper
      Rings, 55
    Spinach Feta Strudel Slices, 64
    Tyropetes (Fennel-Spiced Cheese
      Triangles), 65
Cherries, Pickled, 53
Chestnut Pâté, Artichoke and, 9
Chicken
    Cantonese Stuffed Chicken Wings,
      93
    Cha Gio (Spring Rolls), 95
    Chicken and Grape Salad, 39
    Chicken and Hazelnut Terrine, 21
    Chicken Circassian with Walnut
      Sauce, 40
    Curried Chicken-Almond
      Canapés, 68
    Curried Chicken Pufflets, 61
    Paprikás Chicken-Filled
      Palacsinta, 94
    Spicy Chicken Wings, 93
Chicken Livers
    Artichoke Bottoms with Pâté, 22
    Country Pâté with Bacon, 22
    Crostini al Ginepro, 71

Crostini di Fegatini di Pollo, 72
Chile con Queso, 2
Chinese Beef Jerky, 57
Chou Pastry
    Curried Chicken Pufflets, 61
    Hot Mushroom-Filled Cheese
      Puffs, 63
Citronnade Dressing, 28
Clams
    Clam and Beer Appetizers, 91
    Clams Marinara, 91
Clarified Stock, 30
Cold Mexican Rice, 46
Country Ham with Finger Biscuits,
    45
Country Pâté with Bacon, 22
Crab
    Crabby Mushrooms, 92
    Crab Chantilly with Papaya, 38
    Crabmeat Dip, 5
    Crabmeat Paste, 5
    Filled Tartlets, 60
Cream Cheese and Almond Tartlets,
    60
Crepes and Pancakes
    Basic Palacsinta Shells, 94
    Crespelle with Italian Sausage and
      Salsa Balsamella, 106
    Mini-Crepes with Asparagus, 56
    Pancakes with Seven Fillings and
      Sauce, 98
    Paprikás Chicken-Filled
      Palacsinta, 94
    Spinach Palacsinta, 84
Crostini
    Crostini al Ginepro, 71
    Crostini di Fegatini di Pollo, 72
    Crostino Caldo alla Re Guido
      d'Andrea, 71
Croustades, Mushroom-Sausage, 72
Crudité Salad with Scallops and
    Shrimp, 37
Crudités with Peruvian Peanut
    Dipping Sauce, 3
Crusty French Bread, 74
Crusty Whole Wheat Bread, 76
Cucumbers
    Cucumbers with Mushroom
      Stuffing, 48
    Japanese Sweet Pickle Slices, 52
    Marinated Shrimp and Cucumber,
      36
Curried Chicken-Almond Canapés,
    68
Curried Chicken Pufflets, 61

Daiquiri, 111
Danish Meatballs, 100
Dashi (Basic Stock), 51
Deep-Fried Cheese, 88
Deep Frying Guidelines, 86
Dilled Mushrooms, 53
Dips
    Avocado-Yogurt Dip, 2
    Chile con Queso, 2

Crabmeat Dip, 5
Herb Dip, 2
Lemon-Anchovy Dipping Sauce, 3
Lemon Cream, 33
Perfect Guacamole, 4
Peruvian Peanut Dipping Sauce, 3
Raw Radish Sauce, 4
Refritos, 8
Taramosalata, 4
Dolmathes (Stuffed Grape Leaves),
    50
Duck
    Chang's Anise-Smoked Duck, 42
    Duck Liver Pâté in Port Aspic, 23
    Galantine de Canard à l'Orange,
      40

Eggplant
    Caponata (Italian Eggplant
      Appetizer), 7
    Eggplant Spread, 7
    Eggplant with Prosciutto and Bel
      Paese, 85
Egg Rolls
    Cha Gio (Spring Rolls), 95
    Korean Mondu, 107
    Shrimp Egg Rolls, 90
Eggs
    Smoked Turkey-Stuffed Eggs, 54
    Tuna-Stuffed Eggs, 54
    Watercress-Stuffed Eggs, 54
Emerald Isle Bread, 77

Fennel
    Squid, Fennel and Avocado Salad,
      35
    Tyropetes (Fennel-Spiced Cheese
      Triangles), 65
    Zucchini Cups with Fennel, 87
Festive Spinach Spread, 8
Filled Barquettes, 61
Filled Tartlets, 60
Fish. *See* individual names
Fish Aspic, 20
Foglie de Salvia Ripiene, 88
Fresh Fruit Cascade, 34
Fresh Tomato Sauce, 16
Fried Walnuts, 58
Fried Zucchini Flowers, 85
Frikadeller (Danish Meatballs), 100
Fritters
    Asparagus Cheese Fritters, 82
    Deep-Fried Cheese, 88
    Foglie de Salvia Ripiene, 88
    Fried Zucchini Flowers, 85
    Zucchini Sticks, 86
Fritto Misto, 91
Fruit. *See* Salads and individual
    names

Galantine de Canard à l'Orange, 40
Garbanzo-Sesame Spread, 8
Goi and Banh Phong Tom (Hors
    d'Oeuvre Salad), 44
Goulash, Szekely, 105

Grapes Stuffed with Bleu Cheese, 55
Gravlax, 38
Green Beans, Pickled Dilled, 52
Grilled Mushrooms with Marrow
    and Herbs, 82
Guacamole, Perfect, 4

Ham
    Country Ham with Finger
        Biscuits, 45
    Ham and Fennel Seed Terrine, 24
    Ham-Stuffed Mushrooms, 57
Herb Dip, 2
Herb Dressing, 39
Herring
    Bird's Nest, 35
    Herring-Stuffed Beets, 56
    Quick Glassblower's Herring, 37
Holiday Roasted Nut Mix, 57
Homemade Herb Cheese, 7
Homemade Taco Chips, 80
Hors d'Oeuvre Biscuits, 79
Hors d'Oeuvre Salad, 44
Hot Mulled Cider, 113
Hot Mushroom-Filled Cheese Puffs,
    63

Indonesian Beef Saté, 96
Indonesian Shrimp Saté, 90
Indonesian Soy Sauce, 102
Italian Eggplant Appetizer, 7

Jalapeños en Escabeche Stuffed with
    Peanut Butter, 48
Japanese Sweet Pickle Slices, 52
Jerusalem Artichoke Salad, 32

Kacang Saus (Peanut Sauce), 103
Kebabs
    Bo Sa Lui (Skewered Beef), 97
    Indonesian Beef Saté, 96
    Indonesian Shrimp Saté, 90
    Saté Babi (Skewered Barbecued
        Pork), 101
    Saté Kambing (Skewered
        Barbecued Lamb), 102
    Sirloin Teriyaki, 96
Kecap Manis (Indonesian Soy
    Sauce), 102
Kir Royale with Raspberries, 110
Korean Mondu, 107
Kreatopetes (Spicy Meat-Stuffed
    Appetizers), 64

Lahmajoon (Armenian Pizza), 66
Lamb
    Butterflied Leg of Lamb, 103
    Dolmathes (Stuffed Grape
        Leaves), 50
    Lamb Meatballs, 102
    Saté Kambing (Skewered
        Barbecued Lamb), 102
Lemon Cream, 33
Liptauer Cheese, 6

Maki Mono (Rolled Sushi with
    Gourd or Cucumber), 50
Margarita Punch, 111
Marinated and Pickled Vegetables.
    See Vegetables, Marinated and
    Pickled
Marinated Carrots, 97
Marinated Cauliflower, 53
Marinated Shrimp and Cucumber,
    36
Marinated Vegetable Medley, 29
Meatballs
    Frikadeller (Danish Meatballs),
        100
    Lamb Meatballs, 102
    Mini Swedish Meatballs, 99
    Sweet and Sour Meatball
        Appetizer, 99
    Veal Meatballs, 100
Mini Cheese Balls, 56
Mini-Crepes with Asparagus, 56
Mini Swedish Meatballs, 99
Minted Rye Punch, 111
Mousses
    Avocado and Radish Mousse with
        Radish Pompons, 13
    Caviar Mousse, 18
    Shrimp Mousse with Avocado
        Surprise, 21
    Sole, Salmon and Scallop Mousse
        with Sauce Verte, 17
Mozzarella-Tomato Canapés, 68
Mushrooms
    Baked Mushrooms, 83
    Crabby Mushrooms, 92
    Cucumbers with Mushroom
        Stuffing, 48
    Dilled Mushrooms, 53
    Grilled Mushrooms with Marrow
        and Herbs, 82
    Ham-Stuffed Mushrooms, 57
    Hot Mushroom-Filled Cheese
        Puffs, 63
    Mushroom Caviar, 8
    Mushroom-Sausage Croustades,
        72
    Mushrooms Pactole, 29
    Ratatouille in Raw Mushroom
        Caps, 49
    Slovenian Mushroom Pastries, 68
    Snail-Stuffed Mushrooms, 49
Mustard Sauce, 83

Negi Maki (Beef and Scallion Rolls),
    96
Nuoc Cham, 95
Nuts
    Fried Walnuts, 58
    Holiday Roasted Nut Mix, 57

Olives, Spiced, 53
Onions, Sweet and Sour Glazed, 83
Oysters
    Oysters Aptos, 93
    Oysters Midas, 92

Palacsinta Shells, Basic, 94
Pancakes with Seven Fillings and
    Sauce, 98
Paprikás Chicken-Filled Palacsinta,
    94
Parmesan Rounds, 70
Pastries
    Anchovy Puffs, 63
    Cheese Whole Wheat Short Pastry
        Tartlet Shells, 61
    Cream Cheese and Almond
        Tartlets, 60
    Curried Chicken Pufflets, 61
    Filled Barquettes, 61
    Filled Tartlets, 60
    Hot Mushroom-Filled Cheese
        Puffs, 63
    Kreatopetes (Spicy Meat-Stuffed
        Appetizers), 64
    Puff Pastry Palm Leaves with
        Cheese, 62
    Slovenian Mushroom Pastries, 68
    Spinach Feta Strudel Slices, 64
    Tartlet Shells, 60
    Tyropetes (Fennel-Spiced Cheese
        Triangles), 65
    Whole Wheat Puff Pastry, 62
Pâtés
    Pâté Primer, 14
    Poultry and Meat
        Artichoke Bottoms with Pâté,
            22
        Country Pâté with Bacon, 22
        Duck Liver Pâté in Port Aspic,
            23
        Meat Pâtés (about), 14
    Seafood
        Fish Pâtés (about), 15
        Shrimp Pâté, 16
    Vegetable
        Artichoke and Chestnut Pâté, 9
        Carrot and Spinach Striped
            Pâté, 12
        Vegetable Pâtés (about), 15
        White Bean and Zucchini Pâté,
            10
Peanut Sauce, 93, 103
Peppers and Chilies
    Jalapeños en Escabeche Stuffed
        with Peanut Butter, 48
    Roasted Stuffed Peppers with
        Anchovies, 87
    Spiced Cheese-Stuffed Pepper
        Rings, 55
Perfect Guacamole, 4
Pesto Pizza Bread, 77
Phyllo
    Buying and Storing Phyllo Dough,
        65
    Folding Phyllo Triangles, 67
    Kreatopetes (Spicy Meat-Stuffed
        Appetizers), 64
    Spinach Feta Strudel Slices, 64
    Tyropetes (Fennel-Spiced Cheese
        Triangles), 65

Pickled Cherries, 53
Pickled Dilled Green Beans, 52
Pickles
  Japanese Sweet Pickle Slices, 52
  Pickled Cherries, 53
  Pickled Dilled Green Beans, 52
  Zucchini Pickles, 52
Piquant Fruit-Glazed Ribs with
  Orange Slices, 101
Pizza
  Lahmajoon (Armenian Pizza), 66
  Pesto Pizza Bread, 77
Planter's Punch, 110
Pork
  Carnitas, 107
  Goi and Banh Phong Tom (Hors
    d'Oeuvre Salad), 44
  Korean Mondu, 107
  Piquant Fruit-Glazed Ribs with
    Orange Slices, 101
  Pork Terrine with Prunes, 24
  Pot Stickers, 104
  Saté Babi (Skewered Barbecued
    Pork), 101
  Szekely Goulash, 105
Pretzels, Rye-Caraway, 79
Puff Pastry
  Puff Pastry Palm Leaves with
    Cheese, 62
  Whole Wheat Puff Pastry, 62
Punches
  Bengal Lancers' Punch, 111
  Margarita Punch, 111
  Minted Rye Punch, 111
  Party Punch Tips, 112
  Planter's Punch, 110
  Sidney Blue's Brighton Punch, 113

Queso, 89
Quick Brown Bread, 76
Quick Glassblower's Herring, 37

Rabbit Terrine, 26
Radishes
  Avocado and Radish Mousse with
    Radish Pompons, 13
  Raw Radish Sauce, 4
Ratatouille in Raw Mushroom
  Caps, 49
Raw Radish Sauce, 4
Refritos, 8
Ribs, Piquant Fruit-Glazed, with
  Orange Slices, 101
Rice, Cold Mexican, 46
Roasted Stuffed Peppers with
  Anchovies, 87
Rolled Sushi with Gourd or
  Cucumber, 50
Rye-Caraway Pretzels, 79

Salad Dressings
  Citronnade Dressing, 28
  Herb Dressing, 39

Salads
  Artichoke Hearts with Sauce
    Rémoulade, 32
  Beet Salad, 29
  Bird's Nest, 35
  Cauliflower, Carrot and Squash
    Salad, 28
  Chicken and Grape Salad, 39
  Crab Chantilly with Papaya, 38
  Crudité Salad with Scallops and
    Shrimp, 37
  Fresh Fruit Cascade, 34
  Goi and Banh Phong Tom (Hors
    d'Oeuvre Salad), 44
  Jerusalem Artichoke Salad, 32
  Marinated Shrimp and Cucumber,
    36
  Marinated Vegetable Medley, 29
  Mediterranean Zucchini Salad,
    Turkish Bread Rounds with, 70
  Mushrooms Pactole, 29
  Quick Glassblower's Herring, 37
  Salad Kensington, 28
  Shrimp in Green Cheese Sauce, 37
  Squid, Fennel and Avocado Salad,
    35
  Tabbouleh, 46
  Turkey Salad with Almonds and
    Ginger, 39
  White Bean Shrimp Salad, 36
  See also Aspics; Vegetables,
    Marinated and Pickled
Salmon
  Gravlax, 38
  Smoked Salmon Rolls, 56
  Sole, Salmon and Scallop Mousse
    with Sauce Verte, 17
Sandwich Bread, 73
Sandwiches
  Trumps Herb Butter Tea
    Sandwiches, 73
  Watercress Sandwiches, 72
Saté Babi (Skewered Barbecued
  Pork), 101
Saté Kambing (Skewered Barbecued
  Lamb), 102
Sauces and Condiments
  Caper Mayonnaise, 100
  Curry Dipping Sauce, 89
  Fresh Tomato Sauce, 16
  Kecang Saus (Peanut Sauce), 103
  Kecap Manis (Indonesian Soy
    Sauce), 102
  Lemon-Anchovy Dipping Sauce, 3
  Mustard Sauce, 83
  Nuoc Cham, 95
  Peanut Sauce, 93, 103
  Peruvian Peanut Dipping Sauce, 3
  Raw Radish Sauce, 4
  Yogurt-Horseradish Sauce, 11
Sausage
  Crespelle with Italian Sausage and
    Salsa Balsamella, 106
  Mushroom-Sausage Croustades,
    72

Spanish Sausage, 107
Scallops
  Crudité Salad with Scallops and
    Shrimp, 37
  Sole, Salmon and Scallop Mousse
    with Sauce Verte, 17
Sesame Cheese Crisps, 80
Shrimp
  Crudité Salad with Scallops and
    Shrimp, 37
  Indonesian Shrimp Saté, 90
  Marinated Shrimp and Cucumber,
    36
  Shrimp Egg Rolls, 90
  Shrimp in Green Cheese Sauce, 37
  Shrimp in Red Rioja Wine, 89
  Shrimp Mousse with Avocado
    Surprise, 21
  Shrimp Pâté, 16
  Shrimp Spread, 9
  Shrimp with Curry Dipping
    Sauce, 89
  White Bean Shrimp Salad, 36
Sidney Blue's Brighton Punch, 113
Sirloin Teriyaki, 96
Siu Mai (Steamed Meat Dumplings),
  104
Skewered Barbecued Lamb, 102
Skewered Barbecued Pork, 101
Skewered Beef, 97
Slovenian Mushroom Pastries, 68
Smoked Salmon Rolls, 56
Smoked Turkey-Stuffed Eggs, 54
Snail-Stuffed Mushrooms, 49
Snow Peas
  Snow Peas with Lemon-Anchovy
    Dipping Sauce, 3
  Stuffed Snow Peas, 48
Sole
  Ceviche, 38
  Sole, Salmon and Scallop Mousse
    with Sauce Verte, 17
Sourdough French Bread, 74
Sourdough Starter, Basic, 75
Sourdough Whole Wheat Bread, 75
Spanish Sausage, 107
Spiced Cheese-Stuffed Pepper Rings,
  55
Spiced Olives, 53
Spice Parisienne, 24
Spicy Chicken Wings, 93
Spicy Meat-Stuffed Appetizers, 64
Spinach
  Carrot and Spinach Striped Pâté,
    12
  Festive Spinach Spread, 8
  Filled Barquettes, 61
  Spinach Balls, 83
  Spinach Feta Strudel Slices, 64
  Spinach Palacsinta, 84
  Spinach Timbales with Fonduta,
    84
Spreads
  Angel of Death Cheese, 5
  Baked Brie Spread, 7

Bleu Cheese Log, 6
Caponata (Italian Eggplant Appetizer), 7
Crabmeat Paste, 5
Eggplant Spread, 7
Festive Spinach Spread, 8
Garbanzo-Sesame Spread, 8
Homemade Herb Cheese, 7
Liptauer Cheese, 6
Mushroom Caviar, 8
Shrimp Spread, 9
See also Pâtés; Mousses
Spring Rolls, 95
Squash Salad, Cauliflower, Carrot and, 28
Squid, Fennel and Avocado Salad, 35
Steamed Meat Dumplings, 104
Stock-Based Aspic, 30
Stocks
Clarified Stock, 30
Dashi (Basic Stock), 51
Stock-Based Aspic, 30
Striped Bass Mold with Vegetable Floral Design, 20
Stuffed Grape Leaves, 50
Stuffed Snow Peas, 48
Stuffed Veal Roll with Hazelnuts in Aspic, 43
Stuffed Vegetables. *See* Vegetables, Stuffed
Sushi, Rolled, with Gourd or Cucumber, 50
Sweet and Sour Glazed Onions, 83
Sweet and Sour Meatball Appetizer, 99
Szekely Goulash, 105

Tabbouleh, 46
Taco Chips, Homemade, 80
Taramosalata, 4

Tartlets
Cheese Whole Wheat Short Pastry Tartlet Shells, 61
Cream Cheese and Almond Tartlets, 60
Filled Tartlets, 60
Tartlet Shells, 60
Teriyaki, Sirloin, 96
Terrines
Chicken and Hazelnut Terrine, 21
Ham and Fennel Seed Terrine, 24
Pork Terrine with Prunes, 24
Rabbit Terrine, 26
Terrine of Garden Vegetables, 11
Terrine of Venison Campagne, 25
Timbales, Spinach, with Fonduta, 84
Tomatoes
Fresh Tomato Sauce, 16
Mozzarella-Tomato Canapés, 68
Tomato Aspic with Water Chestnuts, 29
Tomato-Herb Aspic, 13
Trumps Herb Butter Tea Sandwiches, 73
Tuna-Stuffed Eggs, 54
Turkey
Smoked Turkey-Stuffed Eggs, 54
Turkey Salad with Almonds and Ginger, 39
Tyropetes (Fennel-Spiced Cheese Triangles), 65

Veal
Stuffed Veal Roll with Hazelnuts in Aspic, 43
Veal Meatballs, 100
Vegetables, Marinated and Pickled
Carrot Chua (Marinated Carrots), 97
Dilled Mushrooms, 53
Japanese Sweet Pickle Slices, 52
Marinated Cauliflower, 53
Marinated Vegetable Medley, 29
Pickled Dilled Green Beans, 52

Zucchini Pickles, 52
See also Salads; individual names
Vegetables, Stuffed
Crabby Mushrooms, 92
Cucumbers with Mushroom Stuffing, 48
Ham-Stuffed Mushrooms, 57
Jalapeños en Escabeche Stuffed with Peanut Butter, 48
Ratatouille in Raw Mushroom Caps, 49
Snail-Stuffed Mushrooms, 49
Stuffed Snow Peas, 48
See also individual names

Venison, Terrine of, Campagne, 25

Walnuts, Fried, 58
Wassail, 113
Watercress
Watercress Sandwiches, 72
Watercress-Stuffed Eggs, 54
White Bean and Zucchini Pâté, 10
White Bean Shrimp Salad, 36
Whole Wheat Ballons, 78
Whole Wheat Puff Pastry, 62
Wines with Appetizers, 110

Yogurt
Avocado-Yogurt Dip, 2
Yogurt-Horseradish Sauce, 11

Zucchini
Fried Zucchini Flowers, 85
Mediterranean Zucchini Salad, Turkish Bread Rounds with, 70
White Bean and Zucchini Pâté, 10
Zucchini Cups with Fennel, 87
Zucchini Pickles, 52
Zucchini Sticks, 86

Credits and Acknowledgments

The following people contributed the recipes included in this book:

Elizabeth Andoh
Sam Arnold
Patricia Baird
James Beard
Terry Bell
Natalie Berkowitz and Judith Lebson
Ann Binder
Anthony Dias Blue
Nic and Nancy Boghosian
Marcia and William Bond
Leo Bossolini: Leo, Florence, Italy
Sharon Cadwallader
Hugh Carpenter
Curds & Whey, Oakland, California
Terri D'Ancona
Narsai David
Mary Dorra
Robert Ehrman and Ray Henderson
Joe Famularo
The Farmhouse, Oneonta, New York
Barbara Feldstein
Paulette Fono: Paprikás Fono, San Francisco, California
Jan Friedman
Jeff Gold: The Summit, Harrah's Tahoe, Stateline, Nevada
Gerri Gilliland
Marion Gorman
Bob and Beverly Green
Freddi Greenberg
Laura Gulotta
Zack Hanle
The Harvest, Cambridge, Massachusetts
Diane Hill
Mary Onie Holland
Diane Jubelier
Shari Karney
Lynne Kasper
Kay Koch
Margaret H. Koehler
Louise Lamensdorf, Elizabeth McCall and Renie Steves
Rita Leinwand
Honey Lesser
Abby Mandel
Theonie Mark
Christina McClure
Jinx and Jefferson Morgan
Dann Moss

Jennifer Mutch
Michelle Myers
Bach Ngo and Gloria Zimmerman
Judith Olney
Suzanne Pierot
Joanna Pruess
Irene Ravin
Mary Nell Reck
Joyce Resnik
Katherine Robbins
Franco and Margaret Romagnoli
Lisa Stamm and Dale Booher
Horace Sutton
Barbara and Donald Tober
Doris Tobias
Marilyn Trent
May Wong Trent
Trumps, Los Angeles, California
Jan Weimer
Barbara Wicks-Calnan
Mark Wolke and Deborah Kidushim
Janet and Roger Yaseen
Rhoda Yee

Additional text was supplied by:

Anthony Dias Blue, *Wines with Appetizers, Party Punch Tips*
Robert M. Karen, *Caviar*
Shari Karney, *Buying and Storing Phyllo Dough*
Rita Leinwand, *Aspic for Glazing, Molding and Garnishing; Folding Phyllo Triangles*
Jan Weimer, *A Canapé Primer, Deep Frying Guidelines*
Roger and Janet Yaseen, *Pâté Primer*

Special thanks to:

Marilou Vaughan, *Managing Editor, Bon Appétit*
William J. Garry, *Senior Editor, Bon Appétit*
Judith Strausberg, *Copy Editor, Bon Appétit*
Leslie A. Dame, *Editorial Assistant, Bon Appétit*
Maryanne Kibodeaux

Photographers:

First color section, in order of appearance:
Irwin Horowitz, Irwin Horowitz, Peter J.

Kaplan, Irwin Horowitz, Irwin Horowitz, Irwin Horowitz, Irwin Horowitz
Second color section, in order of appearance:
Irwin Horowitz, Brian Leatart, Irwin Horowitz, Irwin Horowitz, Irwin Horowitz, Irwin Horowitz, Brian Leatart
Cover photograph by Irwin Horowitz

The Knapp Press
is a wholly owned subsidiary of
KNAPP COMMUNICATIONS CORPORATION
Chairman and Chief Executive Officer:
Cleon T. Knapp
President: H. Stephen Cranston
Senior Vice-Presidents:
Paige Rense (*Editor-in-Chief*)
Everett T. Alcan (*Corporate Planning*)
Rosalie Bruno (*New Venture Development*)
John L. Decker (*Magazine Group Publisher*)
Betsy Knapp (*Information Systems and Electronic Media*)
L. James Wade, Jr. (*Finance*)
Vice-Presidents:
Philip Kaplan (*Graphics*)
Anthony P. Iacono (*Manufacturing*)

THE KNAPP PRESS

Chairman and Chief Executive Officer: Richard E. Bye; *Vice-President and General Manager:* Alice Bandy; *Administrative Assistant:* Beth Bell; *Senior Editor:* Norman Kolpas; *Associate Editor:* Sarah Lifton; *Associate Editor:* Jan Koot; *Editorial Coordinator:* Jan Stuebing; *Editorial Assistant:* Nancy D. Roberts; *Art Director:* Paula Schlosser; *Production Manager:* Larry Cooke; *Financial Manager:* Robert Groag; *Financial Analyst:* Carlton Joseph; *Financial Assistant:* Kerri Culbertson; *Fulfillment Services Manager:* Virginia Parry; *Marketing Manager:* Jan B. Fox; *Promotions Manager:* Jeanie Gould; *Marketing Assistant:* Joanne Denison; *Special Sales:* Lynn Blocker

This book is set in Sabon, a face designed by Jan Teischold in 1967 and based on early fonts engraved by Garamond and Granjon.

Composition was on the Merganthaler Linotron 202 by Graphic Typesetting Service.

Series design by Paula Schlosser.

Text stock: Glatfelter Offset Basis 65. Color plate stock: Mead Nothcote Basis 80. Both furnished by WWF Paper Corporation West.

Color separations by NEC Incorporated.

Printing and binding by R.R. Donnelley and Sons.